At Issue

Politicians on
Social Media

Other Books in the At Issue Series

At Issue

Politicians on Social Media

Pete Schauer, Book Editor

Published in 2019 by Greenhaven Publishing, LLC
353 3rd Avenue, Suite 255, New York, NY 10010

Copyright © 2019 by Greenhaven Publishing, LLC

First Edition

Articles in Greenhaven Publishing anthologies are often edited for length to meet page
requirements. In addition, original titles of these works are changed to clearly present
the main thesis and to explicitly indicate the author's opinion. Every effort is made to
ensure that Greenhaven Publishing accurately reflects the original intent of the authors.
Every effort has been made to trace the owners of the copyrighted material.

Cover image: Andrew Harrer/Bloomberg via Getty Images

Library of Congress Cataloging-in-Publication Data

Names: Schauer, Pete, editor.
Title: Politicians on social media / Pete Schauer.
Description: First edition. | New York, NY : Greenhaven Publishing, 2019. |
  Series: At issue | Includes bibliographical references and index. |
  Audience: Grade 9 to 12.
Identifiers: LCCN 2018002538| ISBN 9781534503311 (library bound) | ISBN
  9781534503328 (pbk.)
Subjects: LCSH: Communication in politics—Technological innovations—United
  States—Juvenile literature. | Social media—Political aspects—United
  States—Juvenile literature. | Political participation—Technological
  innovations—United States—Juvenile literature. | Internet in political
  campaigns—United States—Juvenile literature.
Classification: LCC JA85.2.U6 P645 2019 | DDC 324.7/30973—dc23
LC record available at https://lccn.loc.gov/2018002538

Manufactured in the United States of America

Website: http://greenhavenpublishing.com

Contents

Introduction

Social media, the internet, and digital media as a whole have impacted every facet of our lives, including how we receive our political news and how we interact with politicians. Although the World Wide Web was made available to the public in 1991, it was not until 2004—when Mark Zuckerberg cofounded Facebook—that online media truly started to disrupt traditional media and the delivery of political news and content. While large media companies like CNN and NPR were covering politics in the 13-year gap between the rise of the internet and the launch of Facebook, the rise of social media allowed political news to be distributed on a broader and faster scale than ever before, making it an unprecedented development in media. Fast-forward two years to July 2006—the launch of Twitter—and we now have the blueprints for how digital and social media turned traditional media on its head, leading to the relationship between news media, social media, and politics we experience today.

Historically, the political landscape was conveyed through traditional forms of media, which meant the information was filtered rather than instantaneous. The president or another political figure would address the media in front of a podium and deliver a statement or speech to the press, which would then need to be transcribed in the form of an article, which would subsequently be delivered to the nation's doorsteps. As media evolved, television stations began to broadcast political content so that people throughout the nation could watch it live, and then reporters and political experts called "pundits" would analyze it and break it down for the general public. But what was missing from traditional media was the voice of the people: a means for public engagement had yet to be made available. Traditional forms of media—television, print, and radio, to name a few—rarely allowed for the average citizen to have a say; this is arguably the biggest void that social media has filled. Like it or not, social media has allowed for anyone and everyone to join the conversation and have an opinion on anything, and with politics being such a heavily debated subject in the United States, more often than not political content appears in social media newsfeeds and timelines.

The current political landscape in America is one that is rapidly evolving, primarily through the development of various social media platforms and the change in the political figures in power, which has led to more media exposure than ever. The current US president, Donald Trump, is using Twitter and social media in general more than his predecessors and at an unheralded rate, driving increased engagement from his followers. NPR quoted President Trump as saying that he acquired 100,000 Twitter followers in a single day. And while one could make the argument that the rise of social media in general explains the increased usage of social media by the president, the fact that the highest-ranking political figure in our country is utilizing social media more than ever is nonetheless noteworthy. In addition to giving people a voice and a platform to speak from, social media has also allowed people who never paid much attention to politics to access information on the topic, making it easier for them to engage in conversation about politics and stay in-the-know without expending much time or effort. Through the use of short video clips and news article headlines on Facebook, Twitter, and other popular social networks, people can scroll through their newsfeeds and timelines and essentially be caught up on all the notable political news after spending only a few minutes reading and researching.

While we praise social media for its ability to keep citizens informed and help spread information quickly, it is important to mention that social media—and the internet as a whole—can also lead to misinformation and false news. An example of this can be seen from various celebrity death hoaxes seen over the last decade, in which celebrities such as Betty White, Wayne Knight, and Jeff Goldblum were all reported on the internet as having died, when they were in fact still living. Just because something is printed on the internet does not make it true, which is why it is important to get news from trusted media sources and to check multiple media outlets to see if the information is consistent. Social media can also cripple political careers when a politician's personal life gets brought to public attention. While social media allows people to feel more connected to powerful political figures whose personal lives have historically been kept under wraps, there have been many instances of too much personal information being shared on social media and reputations being questioned and destroyed as a result. One notable instance of this is former New York Congressman Anthony Weiner's public downfall due to his missteps on social media. This sort of political disgrace raises the popular question of whether political figures should manage their own social media accounts, or if that duty should be left to a team of experienced public relations or social media specialists to handle. There are people who believe that if a politician is not personally posting the updates to social media, then the close connection to his or her followers will be lost, but others argue that is not necessarily the case. There are ways for social media teams to gather content from the politician without politicians having to directly handle social media accounts. So while the politician is not the person physically clicking "post," the tone and message is still coming from the politician. Furthermore, there has been evidence in the past as to why politicians should not be the ones posting on their own behalf on social media, as Anthony Weiner's case demonstrates.

Social media is an extremely powerful medium that allows politicians to connect with the public in a more engaging manner, and it delivers breaking news and other political information to the public in the quickest way possible. As seen over the last ten years, political figures attempt to use social media to benefit their campaign or image, and not all politicians utilize social media the same way. The volume of political content in people's newsfeeds will likely continue to grow as more social media platforms are founded and more tech-savvy politicians take office. As readers will learn throughout this text, social media has not only changed how political news is received, but it has elevated it. Each year, more social media channels and content platforms are created, and as we have seen in the past with former President Obama's YouTube use and President Trump's use of Twitter, politicians will use these technologies to improve their public image and drive social and civic engagement from voters. That trend is expected to continue for years to come.

The viewpoints included in *At Issue: Politicians on Social Media* explore the role social media plays in the modern political landscape. While some authors will argue that social media is ruining politics, others assert that social media simply brings trends that have always existed in political behavior into starker relief. Others argue that social media can be harnessed to improve political engagement, offering suggestions as to how social media can make the process more democratic. At this point it is safe to say that social media is here to stay, and understanding its relationship to politics is a more urgent concern than ever before.

1

The Majority of Social Media Users Are Frustrated Over Political Content

Maeve Duggan and Aaron Smith

Maeve Duggan is a research associate at the Pew Research Center's Internet Project. Aaron Smith is the associate director of research at Pew Research Center, focusing on the internet and technology.

In the following viewpoint, Maeve Duggan and Aaron Smith analyze the environment of political news and updates within the public's social media feeds and timelines. While there is a seasonality to the volume of political content on social media, Duggan and Smith's findings inform us that more than a third of social media users are "worn out" by the amount of political content on social media, while only 20% of people are in favor of seeing political content. The authors also found that the social networks of Facebook and Twitter are the most popular social channels for political content.

In a political environment defined by widespread polarization and partisan animosity, even simple conversations can go awry when the subject turns to politics. In their in-person interactions, Americans can (and often do) attempt to steer clear of those with whom they strongly disagree.

But online social media environments present new challenges. In these spaces, users can encounter statements they might consider highly contentious or extremely offensive—even when they make

"The Political Environment on Social Media," by Maeve Duggan and Aaron Smith, Pew Research Center, October 25, 2016. Reprinted by permission.

11 |

no effort to actively seek out this material. Similarly, political arguments can encroach into users' lives when comment streams on otherwise unrelated topics devolve into flame wars or partisan bickering. Navigating these interactions can be particularly fraught in light of the complex mix of close friends, family members, distant acquaintances, professional connections and public figures that make up many users' online networks.

A new Pew Research Center survey of US adults finds that political debate and discussion is indeed a regular fact of digital life for many social media users, and some politically active users enjoy the heated discussions and opportunities for engagement that this mix of social media and politics facilitates. But a larger share expresses annoyance and aggravation at the tone and content of the political interactions they witness on these platforms. Among the key findings of this survey:

More Than One-Third of Social Media Users Are Worn Out by the Amount of Political Content They Encounter, and More than Half Describe Their Online Interactions with Those They Disagree with Politically as Stressful and Frustrating

The roughly two-thirds of American adults who use social media sites express a relatively wide range of opinions on the political interactions they witness and take part in on these platforms. Many feel overloaded by political content and view their social media interactions with those they disagree with as a source of frustration and annoyance. At the same time, a substantial minority of users enjoy the ability to consume political content and engage in discussions with people on the other side of issues:

- Nearly twice as many social media users say they are "worn out" by the amount of political content they see in their feeds (37%) as say they like seeing lots of political information (20%). Still, about four-in-ten (41%) indicate that they don't feel particularly strongly one way or the other about the amount of political content they encounter on social media.

- 59% say their social media interactions with those with opposing political views are stressful and frustrating—although 35% find them interesting and informative.
- 64% say their online encounters with people on the opposite side of the political spectrum leave them feeling as if they have even less in common than they thought—although 29% say they end these discussions feeling that they have more in common than they might have anticipated.

Many Users View the Tone of Political Discussions on Social Media as Uniquely Angry and Disrespectful—Although a Sizeable Share Feels that These Discussions Simply Reflect the Broader Political Climate

When asked how they view the tone of the political discussions they see on social media, a substantial share of social media users feel these platforms are uniquely angry and disrespectful venues for engaging in political debate. Some 40% of users agree strongly with the notion that social media are places where people say things while discussing politics that they would never say in person (an additional 44% feel that this statement describes social media somewhat well).

Meanwhile, roughly half of users feel the political conversations they see on social media are angrier (49%), less respectful (53%) and less civil (49%) than those in other areas of life. At the same time, a notable minority feels that the political discussions they see on social media are largely reflective of the political discussions they witness in other areas of their lives: For instance, 39% of users feel that these interactions are no more less respectful than other political interactions they encounter. And a small share finds political debates on social media to be *more* civil (7%), more informative (14%) and more focused on important policy issues (10%) than those they see elsewhere.

Most Users Try to Ignore Political Arguments on Social Media as Best They Can; when That Fails, They Take Steps to Curate Their Feeds and Avoid the Most Offensive Types of Content

For the most part, social media users try to refrain from engaging with the political arguments that enter their feeds: 83% of them say that when their friends post something about politics that they disagree with they usually just try to ignore it, while 15% usually respond to these posts with a post or comment of their own.

When ignoring problematic content fails, social media users tend to utilize technological tools to remove troublesome users from their feeds entirely. Nearly one-third of social media users (31%) say they have changed their settings in order to see fewer posts from someone in their feed because of something related to politics, while 27% have blocked or unfriended someone for that reason. Taken together, this amounts to 39% of social media users—and 60% of them indicate that they took this step because someone was posting political content that they found offensive.

Despite These Annoyances, Some Users— Especially Those with High Levels of Political Engagement—Enjoy Talking, Debating and Posting about Political Issues on Social Media

Yet for all of the tensions and annoyances that accompany political debates on social media, some users do see a good side to these interactions. This is especially true of those Americans who indicate a high level of interest and involvement in the political process more broadly.

These highly engaged social media users express many of the same frustrations about the tone and tenor of political discussions on social media—but many of them simultaneously view social media platforms as valuable tools for political action and discussion. Roughly one-in-five politically engaged users (19%) indicate that they often comment, discuss or post about political issues with others on social media (just 6% of less politically engaged users post with this level of frequency). And nearly one-third of these politically engaged users feel that social media sites do "very well" at bringing new voices into the political discussion (31%) or helping people get involved with issues that matter to them (30%).

Frustration Over Politically Oriented Social Media Discussions Is a Bipartisan Phenomenon

Even as their overall political attitudes differ dramatically, Democrats and Republicans (including independents and other nonpartisans who "lean" toward either party) tend to view and utilize social media in largely comparable ways. For instance, they are equally likely to say that they comment, post about or engage in political discussions on social media (10% of Republican users and 8% of Democrats do so often). And a nearly identical share from each party feels worn out by the amount of political material they encounter on social media (38% of Democrats and 37% of Republicans who use social media report this) or feel that the conversations they see on social media are angrier and less civil than in other venues where these conversations occur. However, Democrats who use social media are somewhat more likely to view these sites as useful vehicles for bringing new voices into the political arena.

Political Content Is as Prevalent on Facebook (Where Users Mostly Follow People they Know Personally) as It Is on Twitter (Where Users Tend to Follow a Wider Mix of Connections)

The concerns and frustrations outlined above are occurring in a broader context: namely, one in which political discussions are encroaching into a range of different social spaces. Two of the more common social media platforms—Facebook and Twitter—are illustrative in this regard. Facebook users tend to be friends primarily with people they know personally (66% of Facebook users say they mostly follow people they already know), while

Twitter users are much more likely to follow people they *do not* know personally (48% of Twitter users indicate that most of the people they follow are in this category). And a large share of Facebook and Twitter users report that they follow a relatively broad mix of people with differing political views and opinions (indeed, just 23% of Facebook users and 17% of Twitter users say that they mostly follow people with political views that are similar to theirs). But despite these differences in the social and political composition of their networks, an identical share of Facebook users and Twitter users report that they frequently encounter political posts and engage in political discussions among the people in their networks.

Political Content on Social Media

For several election cycles, Pew Research Center has documented the extent to which Americans are turning to social media for political information and action. The current political environment —featuring exceptionally high levels of interest in the election, partisan antipathy and political polarization—makes for an especially complex atmosphere for today's social media users. The typical social media user inhabits a digital world that contains a wide mix of connections, ranging from close friends and family members to public figures or distant acquaintances. Often these friend networks represent a potentially combustible mixture of conflicting political opinions, and this intermingling of the personal and the political can lead to frustration and annoyance for users as they attempt to make their way through these digital spaces.

The chapter that follows examines the basic contours of how users encounter and navigate political discussion and debate in the context of social media.

9% of Social Media Users Say They Often Discuss, Comment or Post About Politics or Government on These Platforms

Roughly one-third of social media users indicate they often (9%) or sometimes (23%) comment, discuss or post about government and politics on social media; meanwhile, nearly seven-in-ten indicate that they hardly ever (30%) or never (38%) do this. Younger adults tend to rely much more heavily than older adults on social media as a source of campaign news, but older users more than hold their own when it comes to discussing or commenting on political issues on these sites. Some 10% of social media users ages 50 and older often do this, nearly identical to share of users under the age of 50 who do so (8%). In addition, Republicans and Democrats who use social media (including independents and other nonpartisans who "lean" toward the parties) are equally likely to say that they often comment, discuss or post about political issues on these sites: 10% of Republican users and 8% of Democrats do so with this frequency.

Political Content Is as Prevalent on Facebook (Where Users Mostly Follow People They Know Personally) as It Is on Twitter (Where Users Tend to Follow a Wider Mix of Connections)

In addition to asking about their participation in political discussions on social media generally, the survey also included a series of questions about the composition of users' friend networks and the political content they encounter on two specific social media platforms: Facebook, which is the most popular social media platform by a substantial margin (used by 62% of American adults) and Twitter, which is smaller (used by 20% of Americans) but has attracted an audience that is heavily invested in news and current events. This survey finds that Facebook and Twitter users tend to follow a very different mix of people—but political content is equally prevalent for users of each site, and users of both sites are connected to people holding a broad range of political viewpoints.

The vast majority of Facebook users indicate that their Facebook friends are either mostly people they know personally (66%) or are a mix of people they know and don't know (30%). Just 3% of Facebook users indicate that most of their friends are people they do not know personally. By contrast, Twitter users report that their networks are much more oriented toward public figures and other users that they themselves do not know. Just 15% of Twitter users say that they mostly follow people they know personally, while nearly half (48%) say they mostly follow people they *do not* know personally and 37% say they follow a mix of people.

Yet despite these differences in the types of people they follow (and Twitter's long-standing reputation as the domain of news and politics junkies), users of each platform report that they encounter a similar level of political content and discussion. The vast majority of users of each site indicate that they see at least a little bit of political content in their feeds, and about one-quarter of both Facebook (25%) and Twitter (24%) users report that "a lot" of what they see on each site is related to politics. Meanwhile, 6% of Facebook users and 8% of Twitter users indicate that "a lot" of what they themselves post on the site is politically related.

In other words, users of Facebook and Twitter are equally likely to encounter political material and to engage in political discussions—regardless of whether they are on a site where they are mostly connected to people they know personally (as in the case of Facebook) or on a site where they are connected to a wider range of people they may or may not have ever met in person (as in the case of Twitter).

Most Users' Friend Networks on Both Facebook and Twitter Contain People with a Range of Political Beliefs

In addition to being exposed to a relatively substantial amount of political content from a range of differing people, users of both Facebook and Twitter must navigate interactions with people holding a wide variety of political viewpoints.

To be sure, some users have online networks whose political views largely mirror their own: 23% of Facebook users and 17% of Twitter users say most of the people in their networks hold political beliefs similar to theirs. And a notable proportion of users simply don't pay much attention to the political characteristics of the people in their networks: 19% of Facebook users and 37% of

Twitter users say they are unsure of the political beliefs of their friends and followers.

But for many users, friend networks that encompass a range of political beliefs are the norm. Roughly half of Facebook users (53%) and more than one-third of Twitter users (39%) say that there is a mix of political views among the people in their networks. And an additional 5% of Facebook users and 6% of Twitter users indicate that most of the people they associate with in these spaces hold different political beliefs from their own (Note: a Pew Research Center survey of news consumption habits conducted in 2014 similarly found that Facebook users are exposed to a relatively broad range of posts that they agree and disagree with).

[…]

2

Does Increased Use of Social Media Reflect Greater Political Engagement?

John Wihbey

John Wihbey is an assistant professor of journalism and news media at Northeastern University. He is on the advisory board of Project Information Literacy and has published commentaries and articles in the New York Times, Washington Post, Boston Globe, USA Today, Pacific Standard, National Geographic, The Chronicle of Higher Education, *Nieman Journalism Lab, and Yale Climate Connections.*

In this viewpoint, John Wihbey suggests that while the relationship between the consumption of news media and political engagement is well established, the connection between social media and political engagement—if there is one—remains unclear. He explains the challenges academic researchers face in establishing that such a relationship exists. He also raises the question of whether social networking in itself can be considered political activity.

Academic research has consistently found that people who consume more news media have a greater probability of being civically and politically engaged across a variety of measures. In an era when the public's time and attention is increasingly directed toward platforms such as Facebook and Twitter, scholars are seeking to evaluate the still-emerging relationship between social media use and public engagement. The Obama presidential campaigns in 2008 and 2012 and the Arab Spring in 2011 catalyzed interest in networked digital connectivity and political action, but the data remain far from conclusive.

The largest and perhaps best-known inquiry into this issue so far is a 2012 study published in the journal *Nature*, "A 61-Million-Person Experiment in Social Influence and Political Mobilization," which suggested that messages on users' Facebook feeds could significantly influence voting patterns. The study data—analyzed in collaboration with Facebook data scientists—suggested that certain messages promoted by friends "increased turnout directly by about 60,000 voters and indirectly through social contagion by another 280,000 voters, for a total of 340,000 additional votes." Close friends with real-world ties were found to be much more influential than casual online acquaintances. (Following the study, concerns were raised about the potential manipulation of users and "digital gerrymandering.")

There are now thousands of studies on the effects of social networking sites (SNS) on offline behavior, but isolating common themes is not easy. Researchers often use unique datasets, ask different questions and measure a range of outcomes. However, a 2015 metastudy in the journal *Information, Communication & Society*, "Social Media Use and Participation: A Meta-analysis of Current Research," analyzes 36 studies on the relationship between SNS use and everything from civic engagement broadly speaking to tangible actions such as voting and protesting. Some focus on youth populations, others on SNS use in countries outside the United States. Within these 36 studies, there were 170 separate "coefficients"—different factors potentially correlated with SNS use. The author, Shelley Boulianne of Grant MacEwan University (Canada), notes that the studies are all based on self-reported surveys, with the number of respondents ranging from 250 to more than 1,500. Twenty studies were conducted between 2008 and 2011, while eight were from 2012-2013.

The study's key findings include:

- Among all of the factors examined, 82% showed a positive relationship between SNS use and some form of civic or political engagement or participation. Still, only half of the relationships found were statistically significant. The strongest effects could be seen in studies that randomly sampled youth populations.
- The correlation between social-media use and election-campaign participation "seems weak based on the set of studies analyzed," while the relationship with civic engagement is generally stronger.
- Further, "Measuring participation as protest activities is more likely to produce a positive effect, but the coefficients are not more likely to be statistically significant compared to other measures of participation." Also, within the area of protest activities, many different kinds of activities—marches, demonstrations, petitions and boycotts—are combined in research, making conclusions less valid. When studies do isolate and separate out these activities, these studies generally show that "social media plays a positive role in citizens' participation."
- Overall, the data cast doubt on whether SNS use "causes" strong effects and is truly "transformative." Because few studies employ an experimental design, where researchers could compare a treatment group with a control group, it is difficult to claim causality.

"Popular discourse has focused on the use of social media by the Obama campaigns," Boulianne concludes. "While these campaigns may have revolutionized aspects of election campaigning online, such as gathering donations, the metadata provide little evidence that the social media aspects of the campaigns were successful in changing people's levels of participation. In other words, the greater use of social media did not affect people's likelihood of voting or participating in the campaign."

It is worth noting that many studies in this area take social media use as the starting point or "independent variable," and therefore cannot rule out that some "deeper" cause—political interest, for example—is the reason people might engage in SNS use in the first place. Further, some researchers see SNS use as a form of participation and engagement in and of itself, helping to shape public narratives and understanding of public affairs.

3

Social Media's Negative Influence on Politicians

Taylor Allison

Taylor Allison is a digital advertising strategist with Mothership Strategies, a digital agency focused on political and advocacy campaigns. She received her Bachelor of Arts degree in political science and government from the University of Oregon. She is based in Washington, DC.

In the following viewpoint, Taylor Allison discusses the social media firestorm that former congressman Anthony Weiner found himself in when he publicly tweeted a lewd photo of himself instead of direct (private) messaging it. In the days following the social media mistake, Weiner's social following actually increased. Allison also discusses how Weiner's missteps on social media cost him a run at office for New York City mayor, as a fake account was discovered that was being used to send photos to women.

During the original 2011 Twitter scandal, his essential misuse of social media by publicly tweeting photos instead of direct messaging them, caused his 45,100 followers to all receive the photo, setting off a media firestorm. Claiming he was hacked, the social media platform was almost entirely responsible for the speed at which the information reached the public, and therefore the speed in which the photos circulated and got into the hands of the media outlets.

In the days following the lewd photos, Weiner attempted to use the fast paced social media site to his advantage by making jokes about the alleged hacking incident, causing his follower count to skyrocket. He also joked to a POLITICO reporter, "The weiner gags never get old, I guess." When he admitted, however, to posting the original photos, he was so far down a road of scandal and lying, with pages of proof, that there was no escaping the public and media outrage.

Two years after the original scandal, Weiner came back into the spotlight to run for mayor of New York City. At the beginning, the Weiner campaign was quite smart with their social media campaign by using YouTube, Facebook, and Twitter to get their message across, but that all soon faltered when Weiner was again caught using social media under a fake name to send photos to women. In those moments, his social media platform and public relations campaign failed in a huge way, ending any hopes he had of reclaiming his former political campaign. In addition to social media being his own enemy, his public relations team gravely failed to do damage control in attempts to save the campaign. As one made the point in a *Huffington Post* article, "it's almost as if the candidate himself has been handling the campaign's social media work—or, worse, it's in the hands of an intern—because the messages have become disjointed and horribly timed."

The way in which Anthony Weiner used social media and how it affected his term in office and his run for mayor, is an example of the Uses and Gratifications Theory in the Public Relations field. The Uses and Gratifications theory can be seen in the ways Weiner and his team attempted to use social media during his mayoral campaign to reach the young audience through outlets like YouTube. But it also shows how those social media sites affected how people perceived Weiner throughout the scandal because of how he used social media in an exploitative manner to essentially have affairs with young women on the other side of the country. Despite Weiner's personal decisions, this scandal became this public due to the fact that he couldn't understand the importance and speed of social media in today's society and how easy it is to click "share" and give information to thousands in a single instant.

4

How Social Media Is Used in Modern Campaigns

Pamela Rutledge

Dr. Pamela Rutledge is Director of the Media Psychology Research Center. She writes and lectures on the psychological implications of interactive and social media technologies and consults on the design and development of a variety of media and technology projects. She is a frequent expert source on social media, technology, and popular culture for the New York Times, *the* Guardian UK, BBC4, HuffPost Live, PC World, Seventeen Magazine, San Francisco Chronicle, Good Morning America, Toronto Sun, *and* USA Today.

In this viewpoint, Dr. Pamela Rutledge explores Barack Obama's 2008 presidential campaign as the first campaign of its kind to successfully use social media. She also discusses President Obama's use of social media during his 2012 campaign, making the argument that his campaign's effective maneuvering of social media—along with his opponents' inept use of it—contributed to his election and reelection. Rutledge explains important patterns in social media behavior and psychology as they relate to political campaigns.

The 2008 Obama Presidential campaign made history. Not only was Obama the first African American to be elected president, but he was also the first presidential candidate to effectively use

"How Obama Won the Social Media Battle in the 2012 Presidential Campaign," by Dr. Pamela Rutledge, Media Psychology Research Center, January 25, 2013. Reprinted by permission.

social media as a major campaign strategy. It's easy to forget, given how ubiquitous social media is today, that in 2008 sending out voting reminders on Twitter and interacting with people on Facebook was a big deal. When Obama announced his candidacy in 2007, Twitter had only just started and there wasn't even an iPhone yet.

Four years later, the media landscape looks a lot different. There are an ever-increasing number of social media tools and a rapidly growing user base across all demographics. Current measures of American adults who use social networks are at 69%; that's up significantly from the 37% of those who had social network profiles in 2008. And contrary to concerns about social media causing civic disengagement, numbers out of Pew Research show that 66% of social media users actively engage in political activism online. They estimate that to be the equivalent of 39% of all American adults. Like many other behaviors, online activities translate into offline ones. Researchers at the MacArthur Research Network on Youth & Participatory Politics report that young people who are politically active online are twice as likely to vote than those who are not.

In the run-up to the 2012 presidential election, there was lots of speculation about the potential impact of social media this time around. In 2008, McCain's campaign was as social-media-deaf as Obama's was social-media-savvy. Would the Romney campaign be able to compete in the social cyberspace? Would the Obama campaign be able to effectively harness social technologies again?

Like JFK was the first president who really understood television, Obama is the first social media president. In 2012, Obama not only had the expertise on his team, he had an established social media machine up and running. Since social media is about relationships, having a running start building those connections is a distinct benefit. While the Romney campaign was not left in the dust as McCain's had been, they did not achieve the traction that the Democrats did.

Obama dominated the social media space because his team got how networks work. The real power of social media is not in the number of posts or Tweets but in user engagement measured by content spreadability. For example, Obama logged twice as many Facebook "Likes" and nearly 20 times as many re-tweets as Romney. With his existing social media base and spreadable content, Obama had far superior reach.

The real drivers of an effective social media campaign, however, are based on the psychology of social behaviors not the current technology.

Participatory Democracy

Social media creates a new political dialogue. It takes the power of political messaging away from the mass media model and places it firmly into peer-to-peer, public discourse. In the 1950s, sociologists Lazersfeld and Katz proposed a two-step model of communication. Their model proposed that opinions are not formed through direct information from mass media but through individual interactions with opinion leaders who were similar in demographics, interests, and socio-economic factors to those they influenced. In other words, opinion leaders are the people you connect with on your social networks, such as family, friends, colleagues and shared-interest group members. As any marketer will tell you, word of mouth advertising—a recommendation from someone you trust—is the most powerful form of persuasion. Social media creates multiple levels of trust based on relationships. Social media also allows information and opinions to travel across networks, like ripples in a pond, amplifying ideas and allowing each person to participate as an opinion leader through media production and distribution, not just by passive consumption. In the 2012 election, 30% of online users report that they were urged to vote via social media by family, friends or other social network connections, 20% actively encouraged others and 22% posted their decision when the voted.

There are lots of social dynamics that influence people's opinions and behaviors. From social validation to familiarity that turns into acceptance, social networks and the ability to link peer to peer, supercharge the type of self-organizing movement that Obama's campaign seeded through strategic social media use.

Individual Agency

The increasing use of social media demonstrates to people the power they have as individuals to make a difference increasing both individual and collective agency. Obama's group tapped into this increasing sense of political empowerment to generate support in spreading the word, encouraging other voters and raising funds. Social media and text messaging create opportunities for individual involvement that feel personal. Personal encourages participation; participation creates ownership. By encouraging contribution through small donations using the social media and cellphones rather than focusing on the traditional big donor strategy, Obama's campaign succeeded in raising nearly $1billion not to mention the breadth of social capital.

A Campaign of Memes

The immediacy of social media creates instant channels for memes—an idea or symbol—to take hold and spread rapidly. Memes become a dominant cultural event; they frame or even override other messaging. Romney's campaign was hurt by their lack of understanding of both this phenomenon and the fluidity of internet media channels. The most notable meme faux pas was the "binders full of women" remark that started on Twitter and immediately went viral across multiple media including parody accounts on Tumblr, Twitter and Facebook.

The Use of Big Data

A final aspect of the Obama campaign's social media success comes from the increasing sophistication of online data collection. We may equate data harvesting with large online presences such as Google or Amazon, but they aren't the only ones mining user data. The ability to collect and analyze data on a large scale allowed the Obama team to model behaviors and coordinate and target communications based. They could, for example, predict which types of people could be persuaded by which forms of contact and content. The Obama field offices ranked call lists in order of persuadability allowing them to predict donor behaviors and to mobilize volunteers to get people out to vote, particularly in the critical swing states.

Smart Social Media Strategy Matters

As the 2012 elections show, social media is no longer the "exciting new frontier" for political campaigning. Social media is a normal and central form of communications with distinctly different properties than traditional mass media approaches. Obama has set the bar for future campaigns but social media and network structures should be given serious attention in the media strategy, whether it's for politicians, organizations, brands or public service initiatives.

5

How Social Media Negatively Impacted the 2016 Election

Sam Sanders

Sam Sanders has been a member of the NPR team since 2009. He previously worked as a field producer and breaking news reporter and currently hosts a podcast on NPR called "It's Been a Minute with Sam Sanders," which mostly covers news and pop culture.

In the following viewpoint, Sam Sanders discusses the current political social media landscape, pointing out that we sometimes revel in the bitter disagreements that we see taking place on our timelines and newsfeeds. Sanders also touches on how social media helped fuel the fire between the two presidential candidates in 2016, such as Hillary Clinton's email scandal and Donald Trump's refusal to release his tax returns. Sanders asserts that social media aided in making the 2016 election more about scandal and gossip rather than important political issues and growth.

I've noticed two distinct ways social media have changed the way we talk to each other about politics. Clearly, they have changed a lot, maybe *everything*, but two fairly new phenomena stand out.

One happens on Facebook all the time. Just about all of your friends are posting about the election, nonstop. And there are a few who brag about deleting friends, or who urge friends to unfriend them over their political leanings: "Just unfriend me

"Did Social Media Ruin Election 2016?" by Sam Sanders, NPR, November 8, 2016. Reprinted by permission.

now." Or something like "If you can't support candidate X/Y, we don't need to be friends anymore." Or "Congrats, if you're reading this, you survived my friend purge!" Etc. You know how it goes. This public declaration, if not celebration, of the end of *friendships* because of politics.

And then on Twitter, there's the public shaming of those who dare disagree with or insult you. (I am guilty of this.) Someone tweets at you with something incendiary, bashing the article you just shared or the point you just made, mocking something you said about politics, calling you stupid. You quote the tweet, maybe sarcastically, to prove it doesn't affect you. But it does! You tweeted it back, to all of your followers. It's an odd cycle. A rebuttal of nasty political exchanges by highlighting nasty political exchanges.

This is our present political social life: We don't just create political strife for ourselves; we seem to revel in it.

When we look back on the role that sites like Twitter, Facebook (and Instagram and Snapchat and all the others) have played in our national political discourse this election season, it would be easy to spend most of our time examining Donald Trump's effect on these media, particularly Twitter. It's been well-documented; Trump may very well have the most combative online presence of any candidate for president in modern history.

But underneath that glaring and obvious conclusion, there's a deeper story about how the very DNA of social media platforms and the way people use them has trickled up through our political discourse and affected all of us, almost *forcing* us to wallow in the divisive waters of our online conversation. And it all may have helped make Election 2016 one of the most unbearable ever.

A Problem with Format

Fully understanding just how social media have changed our national political conversation means understanding what these platforms were initially intended to do, and how we use them now.

At its core, Twitter is a messaging service allowing users (who can remain anonymous) to tweet out information, or opinions, or whatever, in 140-character bursts. For many critics, that DNA makes Twitter antithetical to sophisticated, thoughtful political conversation.

"Both the technology itself, and the way we choose to use the technology, makes it so that what ought to be a conversation is just a set of Post-it notes that are scattered," Kerric Harvey, author of the *Encyclopedia of Social Media and Politics,* said of Twitter. "Not even on the refrigerator door, but on the ground."

She argues that what we do on Twitter around politics isn't a conversation at all; it's a loud mess.

Bridget Coyne, a senior manager at Twitter, points to several features the company has added to those 140-character tweets: polls, photos, video, Moments and more. She also told NPR that the 140-character limit reflects the app's start as a mobile-first platform, and that it's different now. "We've evolved into a website and many other platforms from that." And she, like every other spokesman for any major social media platform, argues that sites like Twitter have *democratized* the political conversation, helping give everyone a voice, and that's a good thing.

But even accepting that point, and respecting every new addition to Twitter's list of tools, we find a way to keep arguing. Even the candidates do it.

One particular exchange between Hillary Clinton and Jeb Bush (remember him?) illustrates this new political reality. On Aug. 10, 2015, Clinton's Twitter account posted a graphic with the words: "$1.2 trillion, the amount 40 million Americans owe in student debt."

Jeb Bush's campaign replied, tweaking Clinton's own graphic to read "100%, The increase in student debt under this Democratic White House."

Those two tweets seem reasonable enough. But there was more. In response to the Bush campaign's response, Team Clinton scratched out the words in Bush's redone graphic, added its own scribbled letters, and etched a large "F" on top, for the "grade given to Florida for college affordability under Jeb Bush's leadership." The campaign tweeted the image with the caption "Fixed it for you."

And *then,* the Bush account replied once more, turning Clinton's "H" logo, with its right-pointing arrow, by 90 degrees, sending the arrow point skyward, with the word "taxes" printed behind over and over. That caption was "fixed your logo for you."

It was an exchange nearing petty; these two candidates were trolling each other. But for the most part it seemed totally normal in a campaign season like this one, and in the digital age in which we live. Establishment political figures like Bush and Clinton (or at least their young staffers) had co-opted the language of social media and mastered the formats, with all the snark and back and forth that come along with it, and with an extra incentive to adopt some of the meanness Trump has exhibited online.

There may be even more problems for Twitter than what real live people are doing on the app. A recent study conducted by a research team at Oxford University found that during the period of time between the first presidential debate and the second, one-third of pro-Trump tweets and nearly one-fifth of pro-Clinton tweets came from automated accounts. Douglas Guilbeault, one of the researchers in the study, told NPR that hurts political discourse. "They reinforce the sense of polarization in the atmosphere," he said. "Because bots don't tend to be mild-mannered, judicial critics. They are programmed to align themselves with an agenda that is unambiguously representative of a particular party....It's all 'Crooked Hillary' and 'Trump is a puppet.'"

So, if Twitter is a bunch of Post-it notes thrown on the ground, we now have to consider which of those notes are even *real.*

The company would not offer its own estimate on the number of bots on its app, or any on-the-record rebuttal to the study's findings, besides the following statement: "Anyone claiming that spam accounts on Twitter are distorting the national, political conversation is misinformed."

Even if there are questions about the number of bots on Twitter, the tone of the conversation there increasingly can't be denied. A recent study from the Anti-Defamation League found "a total of 2.6 million tweets containing language frequently found in anti-Semitic speech were posted across Twitter between August 2015 and July 2016," with many aimed at political journalists. And a Bloomberg report found trolling on the service is keeping the company from finding a buyer.

Facebook and the "Echo Chamber"

Facebook fares no better in garnering scathing critique of its influence on the political conversation. At its core, it's a platform meant to connect users with people they already like, not to foster discussion with those you might disagree with.

Facebook's News Feed, which is how most users see content through the app and site, is more likely to prominently display content based on a user's previous interests, and it also conforms to his or her political ideology. A *Wall Street Journal* interactive from May of this year shows just how much your feed is affected by your political leanings.

The company also faced rebuke from conservatives when it tried to share trending news stories on users' homepages; they said the shared articles reflected a liberal bias. And after trying unsuccessfully to begin filtering out fake news stories from users' feeds, Facebook has been increasingly accused of becoming a hotbed of fake political news. The most recent allegation comes from a BuzzFeed report, which found that a good amount of fake—and trending—Donald Trump news is coming from business-savvy millennials. In Macedonia.

In response to these critiques, Facebook pointed NPR to a September post from the company's CEO, Mark Zuckerberg, in which he said, "Whatever TV station you might watch or whatever newspaper you might read, on Facebook you're hearing from a broader set of people than you would have otherwise."

In that same post, Zuckerberg also pointed out studies showing that increasingly, more young people are getting their news primarily from sites like Facebook, and that young people have also said it helps them see a "larger and more diverse set of opinions." And Zuckerberg said the company is trying to do a better job of sifting out fake news.

Late last month, Facebook COO Sheryl Sandberg said Facebook had helped more than 2 million people register to vote.

It's Not Just the Social Networks

Social networks are built the way they're built, but how we've used them this year says just as much about our shortcomings as about any particular network's flaws.

Data tracking trending topics and themes on social networks over the course of the campaign show that for the most part, America was less concerned with policy than with everything else. Talkwalker, a social media analytics company, found that the top three political themes across social media platforms during the past year were Trump's comments about women, Clinton's ongoing email scandal, and Trump's refusal to release his tax returns.

"Social media may have played a role in creating a kind of scandal-driven, as opposed to issue-driven, campaign," said Todd Grossman, CEO of Talkwalker Americas, "where topics such as Trump's attitude towards women, Trump's tax returns and Clinton's emails have tended to dominate discussion as opposed to actual policy issues."

And Brandwatch, another company that tracks social media trends, found that on Twitter, from the time Trump and Clinton formally began their campaigns for president, aside from conversation around the three presidential debates, only two policy-driven conversations were in their top 10 most-tweeted days. Those were Trump calling for a complete ban on Muslims entering the United States, and Trump visiting Mexico and delivering a fiery immigration speech in Arizona in the span of 24 hours. Brandwatch found that none of Clinton's 10 biggest days on Twitter centered on policy, save for the debates. (And even in that debate conversation, topics like "nasty woman" and "bad hombres" outpaced others.)

Looking To the Future

So we end this campaign season with social media platforms seemingly hardwired for political argument, obfuscation and division. We are a public more concerned with scandal than policy, at least according to the social media data. And our candidates for higher office, led by Trump, seem more inclined to adopt the combative nature of social media than ever before.

It's too late to fix these problems for this election, but a look to the social networks of tomorrow might offer some hope.

Snapchat has emerged as the social network of the future. Data from Public Opinion Strategies find that more than 60 percent of US smartphone owners ages 18 to 34 are using Snapchat and that on any given day, Snapchat reaches 41 percent of all 18- to 34-year-olds in the US. Any hope for the social media discourse of the future may be found with them.

Peter Hamby, head of news at Snapchat, says the platform is a "fundamentally different" experience than other social media platforms, in part because, he says, on Snapchat, privacy is key. "I think that people want to have a place where they can communicate with their friends and have fun, but also feel safe," Hamby said.

He also said he is working on figuring out what young people want in a social network and how to make it better. And, he said, social media users increasingly want to rely on their social networks to make sense of the flood of political opinions, reporting and vitriol they're being bombarded with. "One thing that me and my team have tried to do," Hamby told NPR, "is explain the election. ... Because a lot of stuff you see on the Web, and TV, is pretty noisy."

In asking whether social media ruined this election or not, I had to ask myself how my actions on social media have helped or hurt the country's political dialogue—what my contribution to all that noise has been. I'd have to say that even when I've tried to help, I'm not sure I've done enough.

Last month, I shared an article about something political on Twitter. Two women got into an argument in the replies to my tweet. I could tell that they didn't know each other, and that they were supporting different candidates for president. Every tweet they hurled back and forth at each other mentioned me, so I got notifications during every step of their online fight. At one point, they began to call each other names, with one young woman calling the other the "C" word.

I stepped in, told the two that they maybe should take a break from Twitter for a bit, do something else (or at least remove me from their mentions). Both responded. They apologized to each other and to me, and they both promised to log off for a bit. One mentioned trying to play a role in creating a nicer world after the election.

I left it at that, but should I have done more? Should I have urged the two to message each other privately, try to talk politics civilly, maybe think about ways to have enriching, productive conversations online (or better yet, in person)? Should I have asked myself if the words I used in sharing the original article helped lead to the argument? Should the three of us have made it a teachable moment?

Instead, they retreated from their battle positions for a few hours at best, never getting to know the stranger they insulted. And I moved on, and just kept tweeting.

But I had to, right? Making the social web nicer always takes a back seat to just trying to keep up. There were more tweets to see, more stuff to read, more internet Post-it notes to throw along our social media floor.

If social media ruined 2016, it's because of that: We haven't stopped long enough to try to sort it all out.

6

President Trump's Twitter Use Is Unheralded

Tamara Keith

Tamara Keith serves as a White House Correspondent for NPR. She's been with NPR since 2009 and also currently co-hosts the "NPR Politics Podcast."

Tamara Keith looks at President Trump's social media use, including his use of his personal Twitter account, which is largely unheralded from former presidents. Keith discusses the many ways that Trump has used his personal Twitter account to discuss politics, call people out, and break news, as there have been many times where the president has tweeted about something that happened before his media team was able to issue a press release. Keith addresses an important trend that we have seen: that each new president uses the latest technology to connect with and speak to the American people.

Three days after winning the presidency in 2008, President-elect Barack Obama held a press conference, taking questions from reporters. Three days after winning the presidency in 2016, President-elect Donald Trump turned to Twitter.

> Donald J. Trump
> @realDonaldTrump
> Busy day planned in New York. Will soon be making some very important decisions on the people who will be running our government!

"Commander-In-Tweet: Trump's Social Media Use And Presidential Media Avoidance," by Tamara Keith, NPR, November 18, 2016. Reprinted by permission.

An unprecedented feature of Donald Trump's successful campaign for president was his personal use of Twitter and it has continued as Trump meets with advisers and potential members of his cabinet. If this continues into Trump's presidency, the method will be new, but the approach will be in line with a long tradition of presidents going around the so-called filter of the press.

Since Election Day, Trump tweeted a list of countries whose leaders he has spoken with before his team sent out a press release.

> Donald J. Trump
> @realDonaldTrump
> I have recieved and taken calls from many foreign leaders despite what the failing @nytimes said. Russia, U.K., China, Saudi Arabia, Japan,

> Donald J. Trump
> @realDonaldTrump
> Australia, New Zealand, and more. I am always available to them. @nytimes is just upset that they looked like fools in their coverage of me.

Trump mused about the electoral college.

> Donald J. Trump
> @realDonaldTrump
> The Electoral College is actually genius in that it brings all states, including the smaller ones, into play. Campaigning is much different!

And, he's repeatedly used Twitter to air his grievances with the *New York Times*. (He calls it the "failing" *New York Times*, though the paper has reported a surge of new subscribers since Election Day.)

> Donald J. Trump
> @realDonaldTrump
> Wow, the @nytimes is losing thousands of subscribers because of their very poor and highly inaccurate coverage of the "Trump phenomena"

Donald J. Trump

@realDonaldTrump

The failing @nytimes story is so totally wrong on transition. It is going so smoothly. Also, I have spoken to many foreign leaders.

Trump hasn't held a press conference since July, instead opting for the more controlled setting of interviews and of course Twitter, over which he has total control.

"I think I picked up yesterday 100,000 people," Trump said on CBS's *60 Minutes*, citing his growing legion of Twitter followers. "I'm not saying I love it, but it does get the word out."

Trump cited it as a method of "fighting back" against stories he considers inaccurate or bad.

60 Minutes correspondent Lesley Stahl pressed Trump on whether he would continue using Twitter in the same way as president.

"I'm going to do very restrained, if I use it at all, I'm going to do very restrained," Trump said. "I find it tremendous. It's a modern form of communication. There should be nothing you should be ashamed of. It's—it's where it's at."

"Presidents want to get their message out, unfiltered by the press," said Brendan Nyhan, a professor of government at Dartmouth College who contributes to "The Upshot" at the *New York Times*. "In that sense, what Donald Trump is doing with social media is not new."

But Nyhan added that presidents have typically also spoken to the public via more traditional means like press conferences. Nyhan is concerned Trump may not observe other conventions and norms past presidents have followed.

"The extent to which he uses social media to attack the media directly could be relatively unprecedented," said Nyhan. "FDR was not giving fireside chats about why the *New York Times* was a failing institution."

President Franklin D. Roosevelt delivered his first radio address, known later as a fireside chat in March of 1933, in the midst of a crisis of confidence in American banks. The purpose was to reassure the public, directly. He would deliver more than two dozen of them over the course of his presidency.

President Dwight Eisenhower did televised fireside chats, held the first televised news conferences and created the White House TV studio.

President Ronald Reagan held prime time news conferences, carried live on network TV.

President Obama's team used social media, releasing its own highly produced videos and posting photos on Flickr rather than letting journalists into the room. And when he needed to sell the Affordable Care Act to young people, Obama sat down "Between Two Ferns" with comedian Zach Galifianakis.

Each president used the latest technology to go around the filter and get directly to the American people in the way that best suited their strengths.

"In a sense, I see it as an extension of what other presidents have done," said Martha Joynt Kumar, in regards to Trump's tweeting. She's a political scientist at Towson University and director of the White House Transition Project. "They've used the resources that helped them win the presidency. So why change."

Last week, when Trump met with President Obama at the White House, reporters who were let in to document the final moments shouted questions, as they often do.

Obama offered some advice to his successor. "Don't answer questions when they just start yelling at you," Obama said before telling the reporters it was time to go.

Administrations have a way of building on each other when it comes to limiting press access. But Kumar thinks, eventually, a president Trump will find the limits of his favorite medium. Twitter is good for announcements and pronouncements— for feuding even. But Kumar argues that it's not so optimal for selling policy.

"People want to see a president," Kumar said. "They want to hear a president. Take his measure and that's not something that's suitable for Twitter. Announcements are, but explaining the guts of policy isn't."

FDR used his fireside chats to explain policy without having reporters condense and interpret his message. But his administration was also the first to have a press pool, a small group of reporters that follows and documents the president's movements. It's something that, thus far, President-elect Trump has not accepted, though his staff said they are working on it. Nyhan said there are no laws requiring it, and public opinion won't provide much pressure either.

"We can't expect the public to be outraged that Donald Trump didn't follow the lid that his staff gave to the media before he went out for a steak dinner," Nyhan said, referring to a recent night out Trump took without telling reporters. "No one cares. The problem is that the principle of elected officials being accountable to the public through the press is one that's fundamental to our democracy."

Trump has only been president-elect for a little more than a week, so it's probably too early to judge whether he'll stick with tradition when it comes to interacting with the public and the press once he's in office.

On January 20th, Trump's team will be given the keys to the @POTUS Twitter account. Though Trump actually has more followers on his own account than the current president.

7

The Decontextualization of Politics in Social Media

Neal Gabler

Neal Gabler is the author of five books and the recipient of two LA Times Book Prizes, Time Magazine's *nonfiction book of the year, and* USA Today's *biography of the year. He is a senior fellow at the Lear Center for the Study of Entertainment and Society.*

In this viewpoint, Neal Gabler argues that while President Donald Trump comes across as the ultimate social media president, this is the result of a mutual thoughtlessness from President Trump and social media users rather than the consequence of any strategizing from the Trump campaign. He asserts that social media encourages the decontextualization of events through cutting them into brief, catchy takes—or "soundbites"—rather than offering the whole story. Gabler emphasizes the importance of contextualizing the news and current events in order to form reasoned opinions on them.

By now I must be at least the millionth commentator to observe that Donald Trump is the candidate for whom social media have longed. What FDR was to radio and JFK to television, Trump is to Twitter, Instagram, Facebook, Snapchat, et al.

This is usually taken to mean that Trump, like some political McLuhan, is a mastermind who understands social media the way his forebears understood their media. But I suspect that with him,

"Donald Trump, the Emperor of Social Media," by Neal Gabler, Public Square Media, Inc, April 30, 2016. Reprinted by permission.

it may be less a matter of his brilliance or even his intuition than of the accidental match of personality with medium. He is a man of his technological moment.

The standard take on that mutuality is that social media prioritize constant churn, and Trump is a non-stop, one-man political tornado, roaring through this campaign and sucking up every news cycle in his vortex. That certainly describes what Trump has done, but it isn't exclusive to social media. In fact, he seems to have grabbed more attention on traditional news sites, especially cable TV, than on social media.

Where Trump and social media *do* conjoin, promoting his candidacy and changing our whole political environment, isn't in the generation of noise. It is in something even more fundamental to each: Trump is the "decontexualizer-in-chief" operating in a medium that likewise is about cutting the world into bits that don't necessarily accrete into anything sensical.

Books have been written about the impact of social media on our electoral process, and decontextualization usually isn't high on the list of transformations, in part because fragmentation isn't usually high on the list of properties that inhere to social media. Those properties, as I see them, are instantaneity, anonymity, democratization, authenticity and yes, fragmentation, and they lead, in their various ways, to a variety of consequences.

Studies have shown, not surprisingly, that social media contribute to increased polarization of our politics, since social media allow like-minded people to find one another who might otherwise be atomized—sometimes to public advantage, and sometimes not.

You might think of social media as a mechanism of social aggregation that can lead to positive social activism. Then again you might think of it as a virtual Munich beer hall. In any case, I don't think there is any doubt that social media have begun to edge out more traditional forms of collective action—for example, party apparatuses. And I also don't think there is any doubt that Trump benefited from this erosion, the darling of social media vanquishing Jeb Bush, the darling of the GOP establishment, or Marco Rubio, the darling of the MSM [mainstream media].

Thanks in part to the anonymity in which folks can use social media, those media have also been accused of coarsening our politics, evicting the politesse, and Trump has clearly benefited from that, too. It is much easier to bloviate, as Trump's supporters do, in the blogosphere where you can't be found than on the page or the TV screen where you can. There are no trolls in the MSM because there are no bridges for them to hide under. (OK, I take that back. There *is* Fox News.) We all know that social media can facilitate bullies and fortify the weak and cowardly, which can be mistaken for the authenticity of speaking your mind. Again, enter Donald Trump.

When you think of democratization on social media, you think of that collective action I referenced above. But social media—in fact, the internet generally—have also recalibrated our focus by democratizing information; not the access to it, but the lack of discrimination among bits of information. The internet is a great disinformation machine where anyone can say anything. It is also a kind of magnifying glass enlarging the most minute and trivial things—things, frankly, that very few people seemed to care about before the advent of the internet. I don't recall us ever having recaps of every episode of every television program, complete with critical annotation. Well, now we do.

Similarly, though live tweeting might be perceived as a form of increased immediacy, it might also be perceived as a form of disproportion. By magnifying the small and putting everything on the same valence, the trivial and the significant together, it fogs our ability to discern the big from the small. And, God knows, this has helped Trump, too. If he is the most bullying of candidates, he is also the most trivializing. His idea of a policy pronouncement is "build a wall."

When it comes to democratization, though, perhaps more important as a practical matter is how social media can allow a candidate to circumvent the MSM and seize the narrative: the democracy of challenging the gatekeepers. This has certainly been one of Trump's achievements as well. Every time the MSM begin one of their Trump rants—the sort of rants that in the past have forged iron narratives candidates cannot break—Trump rants right back over Twitter, leaving the MSM no choice but to cover the rant and, in the process, subvert themselves.

I said in an earlier column that in Iowa, Trump stole the narrative away from the MSM. He has been running with it ever since, and it has been this collaboration between Trump and social media that, I think, may be the second most important way he and they have transformed our political process. By the lights of the MSM, Trump should have been buried long ago under the weight of his effrontery. With the help of social media, he hasn't been.

I say "second most" because the *most* important, I believe, is the way Trump, with the accommodation of social media, has used its affinity for decontextualization to decontextualize our politics. Social media are the champions of the nugget—the minute-or-less Instagram film, the 140-character tweet, the instantaneous Snapchat, the six-second (yes, six seconds!) Vine. Because nothing in social media is sustained, *people* may connect, but *ideas* rarely do. By the time you have finished slicing and dicing everything into those nuggets, you have pried them out of any larger context, any skein of meaning, any argument, any vision. In a way, social media take the *Memento* approach to life and apply it to everything.

Politically, this fragmentation has major ramifications. Context is reason. Context is what enables us to weigh and judge. Context removes impulse. And this is really why you cannot conduct a serious campaign on social media. Context disappears. Of course, radio lends itself to emotion and unreason and even soundbites. So obviously does television. Both can substitute the momentary for the considered.

This is one of the things the great media analyst Neil Postman decried in his book *Amusing Ourselves to Death*. He fretted over the way an increasingly visceral culture had given rise to an increasingly unserious culture, with the obvious political implications. Above all else, Donald Trump is the candidate of impulse running against candidates of calculation. He is the king of the one-liner, the insult, the proudly politically incorrect slur. And that is a central reason why disaffected Republicans have rallied to him. He is nothing but bites. All of which makes Trump not just a more outrageous and blustering candidate than the ones to whom we are accustomed. It makes him an epistemologically different kind of candidate—one who challenges the very basis of our politics. He doesn't have to make sense. He doesn't have to provide a program or a vision. All he needs are his zingers, so long as they are no more than 140-characters. Twitter can do that to you. And now we are getting a taste of what it can do to our political discourse.

8

The Use of Social Media Is One Source of Political Disintermediation

Nilagia McCoy

Nilagia McCoy is the Communications Director for the Shorenstein Center on Media, Politics, and Public Policy at Harvard University.

In this viewpoint, Nilagia McCoy reports on what Nancy Gibbs— an editor for TIME *Magazine—believes to be the key sources of disruption for 2016 presidential campaigns. According to Gibbs' presentation, technology has brought about a great deal of change across a number of industries, and the political disruption only mirrors this overriding trend. She argues that social media is one of the key sources of disintermediation in politics, meaning it brings about the removal of an intermediary like the media and political parties in interactions between candidates and voters. She asserts that social media and technology in general must be embraced by those in politics for them to effectively govern in the technological era.*

Nancy Gibbs, editor of TIME, discussed the parallels between the disruption of the media industry and the upheaval of politics during the 2016 presidential campaign.

In this election cycle, the "traditional entities"—the political parties, the media and the donor class—have been "cut out" as middlemen, said Gibbs. Outsider candidates have been able to "build an audience, deliver a message, and create a platform, all of their own construction." Candidates can speak directly to voters through social media; Bernie Sanders in particular, despite a lack of media coverage compared to Donald Trump, was able to raise millions, said Gibbs. And although he has made extensive use of media coverage, Trump has circumvented both the Republican Party and the donor class.

At the same time, legacy media outlets are no longer as authoritative as they once were. "We are raising a generation now in which everyone is in the media business," said Gibbs of young people's fluency in digital publishing. Editorials, once a powerful tool of persuasion, have reduced influence on a public with less reverence for institutions. Gibbs said of a *TIME* graphic that went viral: "The four-second GIF of the symbol of America attacking Donald Trump is a more powerful editorial statement in 2016 than anything that *The New York Times* or "World News Tonight" or *The Wall Street Journal* could possibly say."

This disruption mirrors a technology-driven transformation taking place across industries, said Gibbs, with companies such as Uber, Airbnb and Amazon eliminating the middlemen and even the company's ownership of goods or property. "Why should the media be any different? I think that that is a bracing situation for those of us who have spent our lives as professional journalists," she said, "but I also think it's a fascinating opportunity, and I would argue a moment for some humility."

"One of the reasons media has been disintermediated is because we have gotten a lot wrong, particularly in this race," she continued. Both Trump and Sanders were discounted by the media, said Gibbs, "because we have systems and rules and arbitrators and power brokers who will prevent anything this wild and unprecedented from happening—that has all turned out to be wrong."

"Change is hard, and fear seldom brings out the best in people or in institutions…it is going to take a particular kind of courage on the part of the press, on the part of the political class, even on the part of voters to explore the new territory that we find ourselves in," said Gibbs.

Gibbs was optimistic that the current disruption of media and politics also brings with it new opportunities. "Never in history have we had the power to reach the audiences that we reach now," she said, also noting that the ability to better tell stories with data and across multiple platforms is another beneficial development of technological advances.

"This can be a golden age not only of journalism, but of governance, because these tools apply every bit as much to those who are looking to shape policy," she continued. "If you are a citizen with a good idea looking to solve a problem, your ability to rally people to your cause... has never before been as great as it is now."

Gibbs closed her talk with some suggestions for how media and government organizations could best move forward, and strengthen democracy. The media need to be willing to tell stories about the ways in which government is working, she said, noting that there is an "institutional hostility" toward positive stories about public figures solving pressing problems.

Additionally, both legacy news outlets and government need to embrace technology, said Gibbs. She described a "digital divide" that exists between the public and private sectors in their leverage of technology. "Every time citizens read about the rollout of Heathcare.gov...or the VA's computers not being able to talk to each other... it is a real problem for the way government and politicians and policymakers are going to be perceived." Having witnessed a similar resistance to the adoption of new technologies in the newsroom, Gibbs said, "we need to be open to the idea that this first generation of digital natives has a great deal to teach the rest of us, in whatever field we are in."

9

Social Media Has Changed Politics Forever

Deana A. Rohlinger

Deana A. Rohlinger is an associate professor of sociology at Florida State University, where her teaching and research focuses on the role of media and social movements in politics.

In the following viewpoint, Deana A. Rohlinger focuses on how the internet is changing politics. Of the three main points discussed, participation is arguably the most important. The internet and other digital technologies have encouraged and allowed citizens to participate in online group discussions and feel like their voice is being heard. Group forums allow for opinions to be shared and for people to learn more about politics and national issues in a quicker manner.

V irtual petitions, online money-bombs, forums to debate issues, and the use of social media and email to recruit people for meetings and protests—all are ways in which today's political activists try to engage citizens and influence the political process. Social movements across the political spectrum use new technologies to effect change and influence party politics, but little is systematically known about how they do it—or what difference it makes.

A recent study looked closely at MoveOn and Tea Party activists in Tallahassee, Florida. On the progressive side, MoveOn

"How Social Movements are Using the Internet to Change Politics," by Deana A. Rohlinger, Scholars Strategy Network, January 2012. Reprinted by permission.

participants are part of a centralized web-based organization that encourages local activists to host events as part of nationwide campaigns. On the conservative side, Tea Party activism is nationwide but not centrally managed. Grassroots Tea Party groups have formed in localities, including three in Tallahassee. In addition to doing participant observation and analyzing media coverage, websites, and public documents, researchers did in-depth interviews with MoveOn and Tea Party activists to gain fresh insights into how they use various forms of internet-based communication to pursue their political goals. The results show how social movements operate in the internet age. By acting nimbly outside established organizational channels, successful social movements have brought the "entrepreneurial spirit" online and into the American political system.

Internet Technologies Overcome Obstacles to Participation

- Online groups overcome well-known obstacles to participation—such as time constraints, lack of skills, and low income. Online movements let people choose when to click; and they usually do not charge membership dues in any traditional sense. They encourage participation in lots of small ways—allowing people to share opinions, sign petitions, ask to be kept informed, and donate small amounts of money.
- Successful online groups use internet communications and networking to teach supporters new political skills and get them involved in the "real world." Models for action can be rapidly disseminated, and people can be given tools to get in touch with other potential supporters in their community. Supporters can be taught how to host political gatherings, organize a rally, and canvass their neighbors online.
- Effective groups use technology to get supporters involved in the decision-making process—for example, by hosting forums for discussion or by asking people to give their

opinion about issues to highlight. This sustains support for a cause, because individuals see the organization as democratic and responsive to their feedback.

Internet Tactics Help Movements Stress Big Ideas and Downplay Controversy

Rather than promoting specialized causes or detailed platforms, technologically savvy political activists focus on selling big ideas that promise to change the world, stressing themes that unify rather than divide citizens from many different backgrounds.

- Movements use the internet along with other approaches to push messages that pit "average Americans" against power holders such as "the party establishment" or "elite Washington insiders." For example, both MoveOn and the Tea Party portray themselves as insurgents and use strong rhetorical oppositions. The internet lends itself to any movement that wants to portray itself as going around or rebelling against elites.
- Successful social movements avoid issues that might divide supporters. Movements featuring online communication can manage what gets featured in their message. For example, MoveOn uses internet feedback to find high priorities that unite supporters, and it also learns what might divide people and reduce enthusiasm. Similarly, Tallahassee Tea Party groups avoid highlighting abortion and gay marriage—"hot button" issues that create fissures among their supporters.

Social Movements and Political Parties

The ability of social movements to leverage internet communication technologies with great effectiveness changes dynamics between movements and political parties in the 21st century. Internet-savvy movements can help fill in gaps in party structures. For example, in recent elections progressive groups like MoveOn.org have targeted swing states with campaigns designed to bring progressive voters to the polls on behalf of Democrats. And Tea Party groups spread enthusiasm among Republican voters in 2010. But at the same time, social movements use the internet to pressure and compete with the major political parties. This happens in several ways:

- Social movements draw dollars away from political parties. Political parties must struggle to represent voters on many issues, while raising money and maintaining broad support. Yet internet savvy social movements operating outside of direct party control can sometimes use a sharper message to raise millions and get supporters involved beyond the checkbook. This may diminish the fundraising ability of political parties. Small and big donors alike turn to activist groups they believe can quickly and effectively challenge established politicians and policy positions.
- Savvy movements can use advertising, earned media, and viral campaigns to build support for their issues and force political parties to take up their causes. For example, since 2009 all Republican candidates and officeholders have scrambled to address Tea Party calls for cuts in spending and reductions in the national debt. Movements have always pressured parties, but movements in the internet era can have a big impact very quickly.
- Movement activists believe that attempts to establish a third party will fail, and so they pressure and work with the closest major party. Tea Partiers, for example, pressure Republicans and compete for party leadership positions at local, state, and national levels; and MoveOn participants support Democrats who favor movement stances on key issues.

10

Social Media Can Be Misleading

Filippo Menczer

Filippo Menczer is a professor of computer science and informatics at Indiana University and is Director of the Center for Complex Networks and Systems Research.

Filippo Menczer discusses how parties that deliver information to the public have exploited social media. Menczer writes about a study that he and his colleagues conducted in which they created fake news and posted it on a website after learning that 72% of college students trusted links they saw their friends share on social media. Menczer also goes into the creation of social media bots, which are essentially fake social media accounts that are controlled by computer software and are made to look like actual people. These are also a part of the social media landscape affecting politics.

If you get your news from social media, as most Americans do, you are exposed to a daily dose of hoaxes, rumors, conspiracy theories and misleading news. When it's all mixed in with reliable information from honest sources, the truth can be very hard to discern.

In fact, my research team's analysis of data from Columbia University's Emergent rumor tracker suggests that this misinformation is just as likely to go viral as reliable information.

Many are asking whether this onslaught of digital misinformation affected the outcome of the 2016 US election. The truth is we do not know, although there are reasons to believe it is entirely possible, based on past analysis and accounts from other countries. Each piece of misinformation contributes to the shaping of our opinions. Overall, the harm can be very real: If people can be conned into jeopardizing our children's lives, as they do when they opt out of immunizations, why not our democracy?

As a researcher on the spread of misinformation through social media, I know that limiting news fakers' ability to sell ads, as recently announced by Google and Facebook, is a step in the right direction. But it will not curb abuses driven by political motives.

Exploiting Social Media

About 10 years ago, my colleagues and I ran an experiment in which we learned 72 percent of college students trusted links that appeared to originate from friends—even to the point of entering personal login information on phishing sites. This widespread vulnerability suggested another form of malicious manipulation: People might also believe misinformation they receive when clicking on a link from a social contact.

To explore that idea, I created a fake web page with random, computer-generated gossip news—things like "Celebrity X caught in bed with Celebrity Y!" Visitors to the site who searched for a name would trigger the script to automatically fabricate a story about the person. I included on the site a disclaimer, saying the site contained meaningless text and made-up "facts." I also placed ads on the page. At the end of the month, I got a check in the mail with earnings from the ads. That was my proof: Fake news could make money by polluting the internet with falsehoods.

Sadly, I was not the only one with this idea. Ten years later, we have an industry of fake news and digital misinformation. Clickbait sites manufacture hoaxes to make money from ads, while so-called hyperpartisan sites publish and spread rumors and conspiracy theories to influence public opinion.

This industry is bolstered by how easy it is to create social bots, fake accounts controlled by software that look like real people and therefore can have real influence. Research in my lab uncovered many examples of fake grassroots campaigns, also called political astroturfing.

In response, we developed the BotOrNot tool to detect social bots. It's not perfect, but accurate enough to uncover persuasion campaigns in the Brexit and antivax movements. Using BotOrNot, our colleagues found that a large portion of online chatter about the 2016 elections was generated by bots.

Creating Information Bubbles

We humans are vulnerable to manipulation by digital misinformation thanks to a complex set of social, cognitive, economic and algorithmic biases. Some of these have evolved for good reasons: Trusting signals from our social circles and rejecting information that contradicts our experience served us well when our species adapted to evade predators. But in today's shrinking online networks, a social network connection with a conspiracy theorist on the other side of the planet does not help inform my opinions.

Copying our friends and unfollowing those with different opinions give us echo chambers so polarized that researchers can tell with high accuracy whether you are liberal or conservative by just looking at your friends. The network structure is so dense that any misinformation spreads almost instantaneously within one group, and so segregated that it does not reach the other.

Inside our bubble, we are selectively exposed to information aligned with our beliefs. That is an ideal scenario to maximize engagement, but a detrimental one for developing healthy skepticism. Confirmation bias leads us to share a headline without even reading the article.

Our lab got a personal lesson in this when our own research project became the subject of a vicious misinformation campaign in the run-up to the 2014 US midterm elections. When we investigated what was happening, we found fake news stories about our research being predominantly shared by Twitter users within one partisan echo chamber, a large and homogeneous community of politically active users. These people were quick to retweet and impervious to debunking information.

Viral Inevitability

Our research shows that given the structure of our social networks and our limited attention, it is inevitable that some memes will go viral, irrespective of their quality. Even if individuals tend to share information of higher quality, the network as a whole is not effective at discriminating between reliable and fabricated information. This helps explain all the viral hoaxes we observe in the wild.

The attention economy takes care of the rest: If we pay attention to a certain topic, more information on that topic will be produced. It's cheaper to fabricate information and pass it off as fact than it is to report actual truth. And fabrication can be tailored to each group: Conservatives read that the pope endorsed Trump, liberals read that he endorsed Clinton. He did neither.

Beholden to Algorithms

Since we cannot pay attention to all the posts in our feeds, algorithms determine what we see and what we don't. The algorithms used by social media platforms today are designed to prioritize engaging posts—ones we're likely to click on, react to and share. But a recent analysis found intentionally misleading pages got at least as much online sharing and reaction as real news.

This algorithmic bias toward engagement over truth reinforces our social and cognitive biases. As a result, when we follow links shared on social media, we tend to visit a smaller, more homogeneous set of sources than when we conduct a search and visit the top results.

Existing research shows that being in an echo chamber can make people more gullible about accepting unverified rumors. But we need to know a lot more about how different people respond to a single hoax: Some share it right away, others fact-check it first.

We are simulating a social network to study this competition between sharing and fact-checking. We are hoping to help untangle conflicting evidence about when fact-checking helps stop hoaxes from spreading and when it doesn't. Our preliminary results suggest that the more segregated the community of hoax believers, the longer the hoax survives. Again, it's not just about the hoax itself but also about the network.

Many people are trying to figure out what to do about all this. According to Mark Zuckerberg's latest announcement, Facebook teams are testing potential options. And a group of college students has proposed a way to simply label shared links as "verified" or not.

Some solutions remain out of reach, at least for the moment. For example, we can't yet teach artificial intelligence systems how to discern between truth and falsehood. But we can tell ranking algorithms to give higher priority to more reliable sources.

Studying the Spread of Fake News

We can make our fight against fake news more efficient if we better understand how bad information spreads. If, for example, bots are responsible for many of the falsehoods, we can focus attention on detecting them. If, alternatively, the problem is with echo chambers, perhaps we could design recommendation systems that don't exclude differing views.

To that end, our lab is building a platform called Hoaxy to track and visualize the spread of unverified claims and corresponding fact-checking on social media. That will give us real-world data, with which we can inform our simulated social networks. Then we can test possible approaches to fighting fake news.

Hoaxy may also be able to show people how easy it is for their opinions to be manipulated by online information—and even how likely some of us are to share falsehoods online. Hoaxy will join a suite of tools in our Observatory on Social Media, which allows anyone to see how memes spread on Twitter. Linking tools like these to human fact-checkers and social media platforms could make it easier to minimize duplication of efforts and support each other.

It is imperative that we invest resources in the study of this phenomenon. We need all hands on deck: Computer scientists, social scientists, economists, journalists and industry partners must work together to stand firm against the spread of misinformation.

11

Social Media Trends Are an Accurate Indicator of Political Behavior

Joseph DiGrazia, Karissa McKelvey, Johan Bollen, and Fabio Rojas

Joseph DiGrazia is an assistant professor of sociology at York University. His research focuses on politics, policy, and information and communication technology. Karissa McKelvey is a software developer, writer, project manager, and activist supporting an equitable web. Johan Bollen is an associate professor at the Indiana University School of Informatics and Computing. He received his PhD in experimental psychology from the Vrije Universiteit Brussel. Fabio Rojas is an associate professor of sociology at Indiana University. He received his PhD in sociology from the University of Chicago and is the author of From Black Power to Black Studies: How a Radical Social Movement Became an Academic Discipline.

Through the statistical analysis of 795 races in the 2010 and 2012 congressional elections, the viewpoint authors argue that there is evidence suggesting a connection between how often candidates are mentioned on Twitter and the likelihood of them winning the election. Based on their findings, the authors assert that social media behavior is not detached from one's offline behavior, but rather serves as a good indicator and predictor of political decision-making.

"More Tweets: More Votes: Social Media as a Quantitative Indicator of Political Behavior" by Joseph DiGrazia, Karissa McKelvey, Johan Bollen, and Fabio Rojas, PLOS, November 27, 2013. http://journals.plos.org/plosone/article?id=10.1371/journal.pone.0079449#abstract0 Licensed Under CC BY 4.0 International.

I s social media a valid indicator of political behavior? There is considerable debate about the validity of data extracted from social media for studying offline behavior. To address this issue, we show that there is a statistically significant association between tweets that mention a candidate for the US House of Representatives and his or her subsequent electoral performance. We demonstrate this result with an analysis of 542,969 tweets mentioning candidates selected from a random sample of 3,570,054,618, as well as Federal Election Commission data from 795 competitive races in the 2010 and 2012 US congressional elections. This finding persists even when controlling for incumbency, district partisanship, media coverage of the race, time, and demographic variables such as the district's racial and gender composition. Our findings show that reliable data about political behavior can be extracted from social media.

Introduction

An increasingly important question for researchers in a variety of fields is whether social media activity can be used to assess offline political behavior. Online social networking environments present a tremendous scientific opportunity: they generate large-scale data about the communication patterns and preferences of hundreds of millions of individuals [1], which can be analyzed to form sophisticated models of individual and group behavior [2], [3]. However, some researchers have questioned the validity of such data, pointing out that social media content is largely focused on entertainment and emotional expression [4], [5], potentially rendering it a poor measure of the behaviors and outcomes typically of interest to social scientists.

Additionally, social media provide a self-selected sample of the electorate. A study by Mislove et al. investigates this bias on the county level, finding that Twitter data do not accurately represent the sociodemographic makeup of the United States [6]. Furthermore, right-leaning political communication channels, such as #tcot ("Top Conservatives on Twitter"), are more active and densely connected than left-leaning channels [7]. Hargittai's work has been extremely influential in investigating gender, income, age, and other social factors that create systematic differences in internet use, including Twitter [8]–[10]. Researchers have also found that extraversion and openness to experiences are positively related to social media use, while emotional stability has a negative relationship [11]. Taken together, these studies suggest that social media provide a biased, non-representative sample of the population.

Despite these issues, a growing literature suggests that online communication can still be a valid indicator of offline behavior. For example, film title mentions correlate with box office revenue [12], and online expressions of public mood correlate with fluctuations in stock market prices, sleep, work, and happiness [13]–[15]. In addition, a number of studies have examined the relationship between online activity and election outcomes [16]–[19]. However, many of these studies have been criticized for a variety of reasons, including: using a self-selected and biased sample of the population; investigating only a small number of elections; or not using sociodemographic controls [20], [21]. Tumasjan analyzed the relationship between tweets and votes in the 2009 German election [18], but these results have been criticized because they depend upon arbitrary choices made by the authors in their analysis [22].

Here, we provide a systematic link between social media data and real-world political behavior. Over two US congressional election cycles, we show a statistically significant relationship between tweets and electoral outcomes that persists after accounting for an array of potentially confounding variables, including incumbency, baseline district partisanship, conventional media coverage and the sociodemographics of each district. These results do not rely on any knowledge of the physical location of these users at the time of their post or their emotional valence. These results indicate that the "buzz" or public discussion about a candidate on social media can be used as an indicator of voter behavior.

[...]

Results

The coefficients for both the tweet and user share show statistically significant effects (p < .05). Each percentage point increase in 2010 tweet share is associated with an increase in the vote share of .268 in the bivariate model. Although the effect size is reduced to .022 in the full model, the effect remains highly significant. Both the bivariate and full models fit the data well; the R^2_{adj} for the bivariate model is .26 and increases to .92 in the full model. The effect for user share is .279 in the bivariate model and .027 in the full model, indicating that, net of all other factors, each additional percentage point increase in user share is associated with an increase of .027 in the Republican vote share. The effect of user share is also significant, indicating that this relationship is not driven by a small number of users. Like the tweet share models, both the bivariate and full user share models fit the data well with R^2_{adj} values of .28 and .92, respectively.

To give a better sense of the magnitude of the effects, an increase of one standard deviation in tweet share in the full model is associated with an increase in the vote share equal to .708. An increase of one standard deviation in user share is associated with an increase of .874 in vote share in the full model. While these effects are much smaller than the effects of the Twitter measures in the bivariate model, modest increases in the tweet share measures still produce substantively meaningful and highly significant predicted changes in the vote share.

There are also a number of significant effects for some of the other control variables that are worth noting. Consistent with previous research, Republican incumbency and baseline district partisanship, as measured by McCain vote share, have highly significant effects in both models [23], [24]. Interestingly, the percentage of whites also has a highly significant positive effect on vote share, even controlling for McCain vote share. This may indicate that voting in this election was particularly racialized even compared to the 2008 contest.

We can assess the limitations of this model by looking at outliers. We examine those congressional districts where the residual was at least two standard deviations above or below the predicted value. We find that districts where the model under-performs tend to be relatively noncompetitive. If there is little doubt about who the winner will be, there may be little reason to talk about the election. In the baseline model, for example, we obtain outliers such as California's 5th Congressional District and West Virginia 2nd Congressional District. These areas lean heavily Democratic. California's 5th has voted Democrat since 1949. Since 2000, every Democrat polled at least 70%, with the exception of a 2005 special election, where the winning Democrat won with 67% of the vote. Similarly, West Virginia's 2nd shows a strong partisan orientation. A single Republican has held the seat since 2001. However, a lack of competition does not explain every outlier. Some districts have idiosyncratic features that merit more research. For example, Oklahoma's 2nd Congressional District is a rural area that has voted for a Democratic Congressman while voting strongly for McCain and Bush.

The analysis of the 2012 US House elections yields similar bivariate results. Data from 389 districts with competitive races yields a bi-variate OLS regression coefficient of .288 ($p < .01$). We observe an analogous effect, with very similar coefficients in the bivariate models across the two election cycles.

Finally, we test the robustness of the results by examining the model across different time periods before the election. Because the link between tweets and voter preferences may vary during the period before the election, we estimate the same models using only monthly shares of Twitter data from August, September, and October. The effect of Twitter share is similar in magnitude across all three months as indicated by their overlapping confidence intervals.

Discussion

These findings indicate that the amount of attention received by a candidate on Twitter, relative to his or her opponent, is a statistically significant indicator of vote share in 795 elections during two full election cycles. Note that this is found in a random sample of all tweets during the first three months before the two election cycles, despite the fact that Twitter has been well-studied as a biased sample of the general population [6]. Our analysis does not require information about the physical location of Twitter users. Further research can investigate why geographical information about users is not needed. Furthermore, we find that social media are a better indicator of political behavior than traditional television media, such as CNN, which many scholars have argued is important because it shapes political reality via agenda setting [28], [29].

The effect of Twitter holds even without accounting for the sentiment of the tweet—in other words, it holds regardless of whether or not the tweet is positive or negative (e.g., "I love Nancy Pelosi," "Nancy Pelosi should be impeached"). One possible explanation draws on previous research in psycho-linguistics, which has found that people are more likely to say a word when it has a positive connotation in their mind [30]–[32]. Known as the Pollyana hypothesis, this finding implies that the relative over-representation of a word within a corpus of text may indicate that it signifies something that is viewed in a relatively positive manner. Another possible explanation might be that strong candidates attract more attention from both supporters and opponents. Specifically, individuals may be more likely to attack or discuss disliked candidates who are perceived as being strong or as having a high likelihood of winning.

The findings also suggest that social media data could be developed into measures of public attitudes and behaviors that could serve as alternatives to polling data. While polling data remains extremely useful, and has seen increased public interest with the rise of popular polling analysts like Nate Silver, alternate data sources can serve as an important supplement to traditional voter surveys. This is particularly true in cases like US House races, where large amounts of traditional polling data are typically not available. Social media data has other distinct advantages, including the fact that, because social media data is constantly created in real time, data about particular events or time periods can be collected after the fact. Additionally, social media data is less likely to be affected by social desirability bias than polling data [33]. That is, a person who participates in a poll may not express opinions perceived to be embarrassing or offensive. For example, few survey respondents will admit that may not vote for a candidate because he is Black (e.g., Barack Obama) or a Mormon (e.g., Mitt Romney). The potential of social media and internet data for capturing these socially undesirable sentiments was demonstrated in recent research on Google searches which showed that the frequency of searches for racial slurs is correlated with a lower vote count for Obama in 2008 relative to Kerry in 2004 [34]. This finding would not be possible with a traditional poll.

Finally, this study adds to the mounting evidence that online social networks are not ephemeral, spam-ridden sources of information. Rather, social media activity provides a valid indicator of political decision making.

References

1. Bainbridge W (2007) "The scientific research potential of virtual worlds," Science 317: 4726.

2. Lazer D, Pentland A, Adamic L, Aral S, Barabasi AL, et al. (2009) "Social science. computational social science." Science 323: 7213.

3. Vespignani A (2009) "Predicting the behavior of techno-social systems." Science 325: 4258.

4. Naaman M, Boase J, Lai CH (2010) Is it really about me?: message content in social awareness streams. In: Proceedings of the 2010 ACM conference on Computer supported cooperative work. New York, NY, USA: ACM, CSCW '10, pp. 189–192.

5. Java A, Song X, Finin T, Tseng B (2007) Why we twitter: understanding microblogging usage and communities. In: Proceedings of the 9th WebKDD and 1st SNA-KDD 2007 workshop on Web mining and social network analysis. ACM, pp. 56–65.

6. Mislove A, Lehmann S, Ahn YY, Onnela JP, Rosenquist JN (2011) Understanding the demographics of twitter users. In: ICWSM '11: 5th International AAAI Conference on Weblogs and Social Media. Barcelona, Spain, pp. 554–557.

7. Conover MD, Gonc B, Flammini A, Menczer F (2012) Partisan asymmetries in online political activity. EPJ Data Science 1: 1–17.

8. Hargittai E, Litt E (2012) Becoming a tweep: How prior online experiences influence twitter use. Information, Communication & Society 15: 680–702.

9. Hargittai E, Shafer S (2006) Differences in actual and perceived online skills: the role of gender*. Social Science Quarterly 87: 432–448.

10. Hargittai E (2007) Whose space? differences among users and non-users of social network sites. Journal of Computer-Mediated Communication 13: 276–297.

11. Correa T, Hinsley AW, Gil de Zúñiga H (2010) Who interacts on the web?: The intersection of users personality and social media use. Computers in Human Behavior 26.

12. Asur S, Huberman BA (2010) Predicting the future with social media. In: Proceedings of the 2010 IEEE/WIC/ACM International Conference on Web Intelligence and Intelligent Agent Technology - Volume 01. Washington, DC, USA: IEEE Computer Society, WI-IAT '10, pp. 492–499.

13. Bollen J, Mao H, Zeng X (2011) Twitter mood predicts the stock market. Journal of Computational Science 2: 1–8.

14. Golder S, Macy M (2011) Diurnal and seasonal mood vary with work, sleep, and daylength across diverse cultures. Science 333: 187881.

15. Dodds P, Harris K, Kloumann I, Bliss C, Danforth C (2010) Temporal patterns of happiness and information in a global social network: hedonometrics and twitter. PloS one 6: e26752.

16. Jensen MJ, Anstead N (2013) Psephological investigations: Tweets, votes, and unknown unknowns in the republican nomination process. Policy & Internet 5: 161–182.

17. Livne A, Simmons MP, Gong WA (2011) Networks and language in the 2010 election. In: Political Networks 2011.

18. Tumasjan A, Sprenger TO, Sandner PG, Welpe IM (2010) Predicting elections with twitter : What 140 characters reveal about political sentiment. Word Journal Of The International Linguistic Association 280: 178–185.

19. O'Connor B, Balasubramanyan R, Routledge BR, Smith NA (2010) From tweets to polls: Linking text sentiment to public opinion time series. In: Proceedings of the International AAAI Conference on Weblogs and Social Media. AAAI Press, volume 5, p. 122129.

20. Gayo-avello D (2012) I wanted to predict elections with twitter and all i got was this lousy paper a balanced survey on election prediction using twitter data. Arxiv preprint arXiv12046441 1–13.

21. Metaxas PT, Mustafaraj E, Gayo-Avello D (2011) How (not) to predict elections. In: Privacy, security, risk and trust (PASSAT), 2011 IEEE third international conference on and 2011 IEEE third international conference on social computing (SocialCom). IEEE, pp. 165–171.

22. Jungherr A, Jurgens P, Schoen H (2012) Why the pirate party won the german election of 2009 or the trouble with predictions: A response to tumasjan, a., sprenger, to, sander, pg, & welpe, im predicting elections with twitter: What 140 characters reveal about political sentiment. Social Science Computer Review 30: 229–234.

23. Klarner C (2008) Forecasting the 2008 us house, senate and presidential elections at the district and state level. PS: Political Science & Politics 41: 723728.

24. Abramowitz AI (1975) Name familiarity, reputation, and the incumbency effect in a congressional election. The Western Political Quarterly 28.

25. Brady H, Verba S, Schlozman K (1995) Beyond ses: A resource model of political participation. American Political Science Review 271–294.

26. Schlozman K, Burns N, Verba S (1994) Gender and the pathways to participation: The role of resources. Journal of Politics 56: 963–990.

27. Verba S, Schlozman K, Brady H, Nie N (1993) Race, ethnicity and political resources: participation in the united states. British Journal of Political Science 23: 453–497.

28. McCombs ME, Shaw DL (1972) The agenda-setting function of mass media. Public Opinion Quarterly 36: 176–187.

29. Roberts MS (1992) Predicting voting behavior via the agenda-setting tradition. Journalism and Mass Communication Quarterly 69: 878–892.

30. Boucher J, Osgood CE (1969) The pollyanna hypothesis. Journal of Verbal Learning and Verbal Behavior 8.

31. Garcia D, Garas A, Schweitzer F (2012) Positive words carry less information than negative words. EPJ Data Science 1: 1–12.

32. Rozin P, Berman L, Royzman E (2010) Biases in use of positive and negative words across twenty natural languages. Cognition & Emotion 24.

33. Fisher RJ (1993) Social desirability bias and the validity of indirect questioning. Journal of Consumer Research 303–315.

34. Stephens-Davidowitz S (2013) The cost of racial animus on a black presidential candidate: Using google search data to find what surveys miss.

12

Social Media Drives More Political Engagement

Darrell M. West

Darrell M. West serves as the vice president and director of Governance Studies at the Brookings Institution. West is also the Editor-in-Chief of TechTank and is the founding director of the Center for Technology Innovation at the Brookings Institution.

In the following viewpoint, Darrell M. West discusses social media's impact on the political landscape, primarily focusing on how social campaign engagement can renew democracy in the United States. West discusses how Facebook serves as a channel that drives civic engagement and how social media has become embedded with political news coverage, allowing for more people to have a voice in political matters.

Social media are the ultimate in disruptive technology. They change information delivery, business organization, online content, news coverage, and the manner in which individuals process new developments. As shown during the 2008 campaign, these digital tools represented a textbook example of voter mobilization and electoral impact. They were, in the words of Engage Partner Mindy Finn, the "central nervous system" of campaign organizations. Using social networking outreach tools such as Facebook, MySpace, YouTube, and Twitter, a number of

"Ten Ways Social Media Can Improve Campaign Engagement and Reinvigorate American Democracy," by Darrell M. West, The Brookings Institution, June 28, 2011. Reprinted by permission.

Democratic and Republican candidates raised money, identified supporters, built electoral coalitions, and brought people in closer touch with the electoral process.

Despite social networking's track record for generating democratic engagement, though, it has proven difficult to sustain political interest and activism online over time and move electronic engagement from campaigns to governance. Faced with a polarized political environment and arcane debates over legislative provisions, many Americans have opted out of the civic participation which was so prolific during the last presidential election cycle. Many voters remain cynical and disengaged from the political process at the very time when the electoral stakes are very high.

This week, the Brookings Institution Center for Technology Innovation convened a distinguished set of experts to offer advice on using social networking and digital tools to reinvigorate democracy and extend electronic engagement from campaigns and grassroots-activism to governance. Participants included Macon Phillips, special assistant to the president and director of digital strategy at the White House; Mindy Finn, a partner in Engage and 2008 director of e-strategy for the Mitt Romney campaign; Lee Rainie, director of the Pew Internet & American Life Project and author of a new study on how people's social networking activities affect their civic and political engagement; and Diana Owen, associate professor of political science and director of American Studies at Georgetown University. We also heard advice and commentary from hundreds of activists who attended the event or tweeted comments during the live webcasting of our event.

Topics for discussion included strategies for voter empowerment, citizen engagement, and governance transformation. Specifically, we discussed: What tools do government and campaigners use to engage the American people, and how have these engagement strategies evolved? How does social networking improve participation, engagement, and collaboration? What role should industry actors such as Facebook and Twitter play in encouraging online civic participation? And how will social media be used in the 2012 elections?

Based on this discussion, we identified ten suggestions for using social media to improve campaign engagement and reinvigorate American democracy.

1. Future Political Effectiveness Is Going to Be Based on Social Networks Because that is Where "Trust Filters" Operate

In a world of information over-flow, it is hard for people to evaluate competing claims. Politicians often disagree not just on interpretations, but on the facts. Increasingly, people are using their personal networks to fact-check claims, evaluate the quality of information, and alert them to what is important in the world. As pointed out by Lee Rainie, director of the Pew Internet & American Life Project, these developments allow individuals and their networks to "act like broadcasters and publishers" and therefore transform the nature of political communications. Those seeking to engage citizens and get them involved in the political process must win the trust of social networks to be influential during the contemporary period. Future political influence is going to be network-based because those are the filters used to access and evaluate political information. Unless you can get past those trust filters, you will not be able to engage the public and influence the course of electoral events.

2. Recognize that Campaign Organizations No Longer Control Electoral Discussions, But that Ideas Come from Grassroots Networks

As Mindy Finn suggests, campaigns in 2012 will be more decentralized in terms of a politician's control over debate topics and more focused around social networks. One of the new ways social media will affect the election is that people are organizing their own networks and candidates will be forced to answer questions they may not wish to answer. Political advocacy should take advantage of these networks to set the agenda and drive civic discussions. This involves everything from the questions that get asked during debates to the manner in which journalists cover the election. Research suggests that trusted news sources are most persuasive with voters so drawing on existing social networks represents a valuable way to affect national conversations.

3. Employ Facebook Comments and Status Updates to Drive Civic Conversations

According to a new Pew Internet & American Life Project survey, 22 percent of Facebook users comment on someone else's post during a typical day and 20 percent comment on somebody's photo. Forty-four percent of social media users say they update their status at least once a week, and among young people aged 18 to 22, that number rises to 73 percent. The frequent, personal interactivity demonstrated by this behavior creates an opportunity for candidates, non-profits, and advocacy groups to engage people and drive civic conversations. Facebook, MySpace, and other social networking tools make it possible to extend conversations virtually and reach large numbers of individuals.

4. Create Virtual Opportunities for Citizen Feedback and Deliberation

In a paper published by the IBM Center for The Business of Government, Matt Leighninger of the Deliberative Democracy Consortium suggests that government agencies use periodic surveys and comment forms to solicit feedback from the public. By asking their views and giving them a chance to provide feedback, this approach engages citizens with government and allows them to help shape the output. Today is the "era of feedback," according to Lee Rainie, and politicians get feedback whether they want it or not. Government agencies and political candidates should be encouraged to develop feedback mechanisms that allow American voters to talk back to political elites. One of the most worrisome developments in the contemporary period is the massive citizen disengagement from politics and feeling of alienation on the part of voters. Social media offer ways to re-connect citizens and leaders, and create more of a sense of public responsiveness and accountability.

5. Embed Social Media Commentary in News Coverage

White House Director of Digital Strategy Macon Phillips argues that social media create a new model of civic engagement that blends traditional with social media. Increasingly, he points out, reporters are following Twitter, Facebook, and YouTube, and incorporating the voices of ordinary people in news reporting. This enhances democratic conversation and gives citizens more of a voice in national debates. It makes news coverage more authentic because it is based on what people say and it weakens the power of the D.C.-based punditrocracy.

6. Use Social Media for Direct Persuasion

The Pew Internet & American Life project survey found at the time of the 2010 election that 23 percent of Americans "had tried to convince someone to vote for a specific candidate" and 10 percent "had attended a political rally." With the help of social media, ordinary citizens can become agents of persuasion and leverage their personal network for whatever values, issue positions, or ideological stances that they cherish. There is no reason why 2012 should not be an engaging election. With the issues we face in the areas of budget deficits, taxes, health care, education, energy, and foreign policy, we should use digital technology to involve people in the campaign.

7. Leverage Civics Education for Political Action and Confidence-Building

Georgetown Government Professor Diana Owens notes that 20 percent of Americans use social media for electoral purposes, but this number rises to 34 percent if the individual has had a civics class or is exposed to instructional material about democracy. She points out that the quality of instruction matters. Courses which integrate problem-solving and collaboration in the curriculum create more political agency on the part of voters and build confidence about taking part in electoral affairs.

8. Improve the Diversity of Information Dissemination and Exposure Through Social Media

No longer does politics have to be an echo chamber where people of like-mindedness listen to one another, but digital technology enriches political conversation and engagement. People are exposed to more views than in the past, according to Mindy Finn. This enriches national dialogues and allows people to get the kind of information that helps them evaluate candidates and policy ideas.

9. Create New Opportunities for Engagement Through Mobile Communications

Smart phones enable activists to reach an entirely new audience and involve them in the political process. According to surveys undertaken by the Pew Internet & American Life Project, 26 percent of Americans used mobile devices at the time of the 2010 election. By enabling people to access information and social networks on the go, this technology speeds up the news cycle and places more of a premium on electronic resources. This includes information from policy briefs and videos to online advertisements.

10. Geo-Location and Behavioral Advertising Allow Activists To Reach People Efficiently and Effectively

Geo-location and behavioral advertising improve targeting and offer greater potential for delivering relevant material. This will allow candidates and activists to be more effective in their resources and provide material that is relevant to people's concerns. Rather than dumping information on people who do not want or trust the material, advocates can target resources more efficiently and effectively, and become more influential at the same time. It is unclear, however, how much tolerance voters have for targeting based on these tools due to privacy concerns.

13

The Media No Longer Breaks Political News

Lumen Learning

Lumen Learning is an open educational resources platform that aids educational institutions by allowing them to cut back on the costs of textbooks while improving student success.

The following viewpoint explains how the mass media covers politics, largely focusing on the bias that it can sometimes project on its news coverage. Lumen Learning presents a study on the 2012 presidential election that analyzes the coverage of major media outlets: CNN, MSNBC, and Fox News. The study found that the majority of content covering Mitt Romney was highly negative on MSNBC, while the majority of Fox News' coverage of Barack Obama was negative information. Overall, after reading through this text, readers should understand why social media and the internet allow for more unbiased news coverage and general discussion.

I n what ways can the media affect society and government? The media's primary duty is to present us with information and alert us when important events occur. This information may affect what we think and the actions we take. The media can also place pressure on government to act by signaling a need for intervention or showing that citizens want change. For these reasons, the quality of the media's coverage matters.

"The Impact of the Media," Lumen Learning. https://courses.lumenlearning.com/amgovernment/chapter/the-impact-of-the-media/. Licensed Under CC BY 4.0 International.

Media Effects and Bias

Concerns about the effects of media on consumers and the existence and extent of media bias go back to the 1920s. Reporter and commentator Walter Lippmann noted that citizens have limited personal experience with government and the world and posited that the media, through their stories, place ideas in citizens' minds. These ideas become part of the citizens' frame of reference and affect their decisions. Lippmann's statements led to the hypodermic theory, which argues that information is "shot" into the receiver's mind and readily accepted.[1]

Yet studies in the 1930s and 1940s found that information was transmitted in two steps, with one person reading the news and then sharing the information with friends. People listened to their friends, but not to those with whom they disagreed. The newspaper's effect was thus diminished through conversation. This discovery led to the minimal effects theory, which argues the media have little effect on citizens and voters.[2]

By the 1970s, a new idea, the cultivation theory, hypothesized that media develop a person's view of the world by presenting a perceived reality.[3] What we see on a regular basis is our reality. Media can then set norms for readers and viewers by choosing what is covered or discussed.

In the end, the consensus among observers is that media have some effect, even if the effect is subtle. This raises the question of how the media, even general newscasts, can affect citizens. One of the ways is through framing: the creation of a narrative, or context, for a news story. The news often uses frames to place a story in a context so the reader understands its importance or relevance. Yet, at the same time, framing affects the way the reader or viewer processes the story.

Episodic framing occurs when a story focuses on isolated details or specifics rather than looking broadly at a whole issue. *Thematic framing* takes a broad look at an issue and skips numbers or details. It looks at how the issue has changed over a long period of time and what has led to it. For example, a large, urban city is dealing with the problem of an increasing homeless population, and the city has suggested ways to improve the situation. If journalists focus on the immediate statistics, report the current percentage of homeless people, interview a few, and look at the city's current investment in a homeless shelter, the coverage is episodic. If they look at homelessness as a problem increasing everywhere, examine the reasons people become homeless, and discuss the trends in cities' attempts to solve the problem, the coverage is thematic. Episodic frames may create more sympathy, while a thematic frame may leave the reader or viewer emotionally disconnected and less sympathetic.

Framing can also affect the way we see race, socioeconomics, or other generalizations. For this reason, it is linked to priming: when media coverage predisposes the viewer or reader to a particular perspective on a subject or issue. If a newspaper article focuses on unemployment, struggling industries, and jobs moving overseas, the reader will have a negative opinion about the economy. If then asked whether he or she approves of the president's job performance, the reader is primed to say no. Readers and viewers are able to fight priming effects if they are aware of them or have prior information about the subject.

Coverage Effects on Governance and Campaigns

When it is spotty, the media's coverage of campaigns and government can sometimes affect the way government operates and the success of candidates. In 1972, for instance, the McGovern-Fraser reforms created a voter-controlled primary system, so party leaders no longer pick the presidential candidates. Now the media are seen as kingmakers and play a strong role in influencing who will become the Democratic and Republican nominees in presidential elections. They can discuss the candidates' messages, vet their credentials, carry sound bites of their speeches, and conduct interviews. The candidates with the most media coverage build momentum and do well in the first few primaries and caucuses. This, in turn, leads to more media coverage, more momentum, and eventually a winning candidate. Thus, candidates need the media.

In the 1980s, campaigns learned that tight control on candidate information created more favorable media coverage. In the presidential election of 1984, candidates Ronald Reagan and George H. W. Bush began using an issue-of-the-day strategy, providing quotes and material on only one topic each day. This strategy limited what journalists could cover because they had only limited quotes and sound bites to use in their reports. In 1992, both Bush's and Bill Clinton's campaigns maintained their carefully drawn candidate images by also limiting photographers and television journalists to photo opportunities at rallies and campaign venues. The constant control of the media became known as the "bubble," and journalists were less effective when they were in the campaign's bubble. Reporters complained this coverage was campaign advertising rather than journalism, and a new model emerged with the 1996 election.[4]

Campaign coverage now focuses on the spectacle of the season, rather than providing information about the candidates. Colorful personalities, strange comments, lapse of memories, and embarrassing revelations are more likely to get air time than the candidates' issue positions. Candidate Donald Trump may be the best example of shallower press coverage of a presidential election. Some argue that newspapers and news programs are limiting the space they allot to discussion of the campaigns.[5] Others argue that citizens want to see updates on the race and electoral drama, not boring issue positions or substantive reporting.[6] It may also be that journalists have tired of the information games played by politicians and have taken back control of the news cycles.[7]

All these factors have likely led to the shallow press coverage we see today, sometimes dubbed *pack journalism* because journalists follow one another rather than digging for their own stories. Television news discusses the strategies and blunders of the election, with colorful examples. Newspapers focus on polls. In an analysis of the 2012 election, Pew Research found that

64 percent of stories and coverage focused on campaign strategy. Only 9 percent covered domestic issue positions; 6 percent covered the candidates' public records; and, 1 percent covered their foreign policy positions.[8]

For better or worse, coverage of the candidates' statements get less air time on radio and television, and sound bites, or clips, of their speeches have become even shorter. In 1968, the average sound bite from Richard Nixon was 42.3 seconds, while a recent study of television coverage found that sound bites had decreased to only eight seconds in the 2004 election.[9]

The clips chosen to air were attacks on opponents 40 percent of the time. Only 30 percent contained information about the candidate's issues or events. The study also found the news showed images of the candidates, but for an average of only twenty-five seconds while the newscaster discussed the stories.[10] This study supports the argument that shrinking sound bites are a way for journalists to control the story and add their own analysis rather than just report on it.[11]

Candidates are given a few minutes to try to argue their side of an issue, but some say television focuses on the argument rather than on information. In 2004, Jon Stewart of Comedy Central's *The Daily Show* began attacking the CNN program *Crossfire* for being theater, saying the hosts engaged in reactionary and partisan arguing rather than true debating.[12] Some of Stewart's criticisms resonated, even with host Paul Begala, and *Crossfire* was later pulled from the air.[13]

The media's discussion of campaigns has also grown negative. Although biased campaign coverage dates back to the period of the partisan press, the increase in the number of cable news stations has made the problem more visible. Stations like FOX News and MSNBC are overt in their use of bias in framing stories. During the 2012 campaign, seventy-one of seventy-four MSNBC stories about Mitt Romney were highly negative, while FOX News' coverage of Obama had forty-six out of fifty-two stories with negative information. The major networks—ABC, CBS, and

NBC—were somewhat more balanced, yet the overall coverage of both candidates tended to be negative.[14]

Due in part to the lack of substantive media coverage, campaigns increasingly use social media to relay their message. Candidates can create their own sites and pages and try to spread news through supporters to the undecided. In 2012, both Romney and Obama maintained Facebook, Twitter, and YouTube accounts to provide information to voters. Yet, on social media, candidates still need to combat negativity, from both the opposition and supporters. Stories about Romney that appeared in the mainstream media were negative 38 percent of the time, while his coverage in Facebook news was negative 62 percent of the time and 58 percent of the time on Twitter.[15]

Once candidates are in office, the chore of governing begins, with the added weight of media attention. Historically, if presidents were unhappy with their press coverage, they used personal and professional means to change its tone. Franklin D. Roosevelt, for example, was able to keep journalists from printing stories through gentleman's agreements, loyalty, and the provision of additional information, sometimes off the record. The journalists then wrote positive stories, hoping to keep the president as a source. John F. Kennedy hosted press conferences twice a month and opened the floor for questions from journalists, in an effort to keep press coverage positive.[16]

When presidents and other members of the White House are not forthcoming with information, journalists must press for answers. Dan Rather, a journalist for CBS, regularly sparred with presidents in an effort to get information. When Rather interviewed Richard Nixon about Vietnam and Watergate, Nixon was hostile and uncomfortable.[17]

In a 1988 interview with then-vice president George H. W. Bush, Bush accused Rather of being argumentative about the possible cover-up of a secret arms sale with Iran:

Rather: I don't want to be argumentative, Mr. Vice President.

Bush: You do, Dan.

Rather: No—no, sir, I don't.

Bush: This is not a great night, because I want to talk about
why I want to be president, why those 41 percent of the
people are supporting me. And I don't think it's fair to judge
my whole career by a rehash of Iran. How would you like
it if I judged your career by those seven minutes when you
walked off the set in New York?[18]

Cabinet secretaries and other appointees also talk with the
press, sometimes making for conflicting messages. The creation
of the position of press secretary and the White House Office of
Communications both stemmed from the need to send a cohesive
message from the executive branch. Currently, the White House
controls the information coming from the executive branch
through the Office of Communications and decides who will meet
with the press and what information will be given.

But stories about the president often examine personality, or
the president's ability to lead the country, deal with Congress, or
respond to national and international events. They are less likely
to cover the president's policies or agendas without a lot of effort
on the president's behalf.[19]

When Obama first entered office in 2009, journalists focused
on his battles with Congress, critiquing his leadership style and
inability to work with Representative Nancy Pelosi, then Speaker
of the House. To gain attention for his policies, specifically the
American Recovery and Reinvestment Act (ARRA), Obama began
traveling the United States to draw the media away from Congress
and encourage discussion of his economic stimulus package.
Once the ARRA had been passed, Obama began travelling again,
speaking locally about why the country needed the Affordable Care
Act and guiding media coverage to promote support for the act.[20]

Congressional representatives have a harder time attracting media attention for their policies. House and Senate members who use the media well, either to help their party or to show expertise in an area, may increase their power within Congress, which helps them bargain for fellow legislators' votes. Senators and high-ranking House members may also be invited to appear on cable news programs as guests, where they may gain some media support for their policies. Yet, overall, because there are so many members of Congress, and therefore so many agendas, it is harder for individual representatives to draw media coverage.[21]

It is less clear, however, whether media coverage of an issue leads Congress to make policy, or whether congressional policymaking leads the media to cover policy. In the 1970s, Congress investigated ways to stem the number of drug-induced deaths and crimes. As congressional meetings dramatically increased, the press was slow to cover the topic. The number of hearings was at its highest from 1970 to 1982, yet media coverage did not rise to the same level until 1984.[22] Subsequent hearings and coverage led to national policies like DARE and First Lady Nancy Reagan's "Just Say No" campaign.

Later studies of the media's effect on both the president and Congress report that the media has a stronger agenda-setting effect on the president than on Congress. What the media choose to cover affects what the president thinks is important to voters, and these issues were often of national importance. The media's effect on Congress was limited, however, and mostly extended to local issues like education or child and elder abuse.[23] If the media are discussing a topic, chances are a member of Congress has already submitted a relevant bill, and it is waiting in committee.

Coverage Effects on Society

The media choose what they want to discuss. This agenda setting creates a reality for voters and politicians that affects the way people think, act, and vote. Even if the crime rate is going down, for instance, citizens accustomed to reading stories about assault and other offenses still perceive crime to be an issue.[24]

Studies have also found that the media's portrayal of race is flawed, especially in coverage of crime and poverty. One study revealed that local news shows were more likely to show pictures of criminals when they were African American, so they overrepresented blacks as perpetrators and whites as victims.[25] A second study found a similar pattern in which Latinos were underrepresented as victims of crime and as police officers, while whites were overrepresented as both.[26] Voters were thus more likely to assume that most criminals are black and most victims and police officers are white, even though the numbers do not support those assumptions.

Network news similarly misrepresents the victims of poverty by using more images of blacks than whites in its segments. Viewers in a study were left believing African Americans were the majority of the unemployed and poor, rather than seeing the problem as one faced by many races.[27]

The misrepresentation of race is not limited to news coverage, however. A study of images printed in national magazines, like *Time* and *Newsweek*, found they also misrepresented race and poverty. The magazines were more likely to show images of young African Americans when discussing poverty and excluded the elderly and the young, as well as whites and Latinos, which is the true picture of poverty.[28]

Racial framing, even if unintentional, affects perceptions and policies. If viewers are continually presented with images of African Americans as criminals, there is an increased chance they will perceive members of this group as violent or aggressive.[29] The perception that most recipients of welfare are working-age African Americans may have led some citizens to vote for candidates who promised to reduce welfare benefits.[30] When survey respondents were shown a story of a white unemployed individual, 71 percent listed unemployment as one of the top three problems facing the United States, while only 53 percent did so if the story was about an unemployed African American.[31]

Word choice may also have a priming effect. News organizations like the *Los Angeles Times* and the Associated Press no longer use the phrase "illegal immigrant" to describe undocumented residents. This may be due to the desire to create a "sympathetic" frame for the immigration situation rather than a "threat" frame.[32]

Media coverage of women has been similarly biased. Most journalists in the early 1900s were male, and women's issues were not part of the newsroom discussion. As journalist Kay Mills put it, the women's movement of the 1960s and 1970s was about raising awareness of the problems of equality, but writing about rallies "was like trying to nail Jell-O to the wall."[33] Most politicians, business leaders, and other authority figures were male, and editors' reactions to the stories were lukewarm. The lack of women in the newsroom, politics, and corporate leadership encouraged silence.[34]

In 1976, journalist Barbara Walters became the first female coanchor on a network news show, *The ABC Evening News*. She was met with great hostility from her coanchor Harry Reasoner and received critical coverage from the press.[35] On newspaper staffs, women reported having to fight for assignments to well-published beats, or to be assigned areas or topics, such as the economy or politics, that were normally reserved for male journalists. Once female journalists held these assignments, they feared writing about women's issues. Would it make them appear weak? Would they be taken from their coveted beats?[36]

This apprehension allowed poor coverage of women and the women's movement to continue until women were better represented as journalists and as editors. Strength of numbers allowed them to be confident when covering issues like health care, childcare, and education.[37]

The media's historically uneven coverage of women continues in its treatment of female candidates. Early coverage was sparse. The stories that did appear often discussed the candidate's viability, or ability to win, rather than her stand on the issues.[38]

Women were seen as a novelty rather than as serious contenders who needed to be vetted and discussed. Modern media coverage has changed slightly. One study found that female candidates receive more favorable coverage than in prior generations, especially if they are incumbents.[39] Yet a different study found that while there was increased coverage for female candidates, it was often negative.[40] And it did not include Latina candidates.[41] Without coverage, they are less likely to win.

The historically negative media coverage of female candidates has had another concrete effect: Women are less likely than men to run for office. One common reason is the effect negative media coverage has on families.[42] Many women do not wish to expose their children or spouses to criticism.[43]

In 2008, the nomination of Sarah Palin as Republican candidate John McCain's running mate validated this concern. Some articles focused on her qualifications to be a potential future president or her record on the issues. But others questioned whether she had the right to run for office, given she had young children, one of whom has developmental disabilities.[44] Her daughter, Bristol, was criticized for becoming pregnant while unmarried.[45] Her husband was called cheap for failing to buy her a high-priced wedding ring.[46] Even when candidates ask that children and families be off-limits, the press rarely honors the requests. So women with young children may wait until their children are grown before running for office, if they choose to run at all.

Summary

Writers began to formally study media bias in the 1920s. Initially, the press was seen as being able to place information in our minds, but later research found that the media have a minimal effect on recipients. A more recent theory is that the media cultivates our reality by presenting information that creates our perceptions of the world. The media does have the ability to frame what it presents, and it can also prime citizens to think a particular way, which changes how they react to new information.

The media's coverage of electoral candidates has increasingly become analysis rather than reporting. Sound bites from candidates are shorter. The press now provides horse-race coverage on the campaigns rather than in-depth coverage on candidates and their positions, forcing voters to look for other sources, like social media, for information. Current coverage of the government focuses more on what the president does than on presidential policies. Congress, on the other hand, is rarely affected by the media. Most topics discussed by the media are already being discussed by members of Congress or its committees.

The media frame discussions and choose pictures, information, and video to support stories, which may affect the way people vote on social policy and in elections.

Notes

1, Walter Lippmann. 1922. *Public Opinion.* http://xroads.virginia.edu/~hyper/Lippman/contents.html (August 29, 2015).

2. Bernard Berelson, Paul Lazarsfeld, and William McPhee. 1954. *Voting.* Chicago: University of Chicago Press.

3. George Gerbner, Larry Gross, Michael Morgan, Nancy Signorielli, and Marilyn Jackson-Beeck. 1979. "The Demonstration of Power: Violence Profile," *Journal of Communication 29, No.*10: 177–196.

4. Elizabeth A. Skewes. 2007. *Message Control: How News Is Made on the Presidential Campaign Trail.* Maryland: Rowman & Littlefield, 79.

5. Stephen Farnsworth and S. Robert Lichter. 2012. "Authors' Response: Improving News Coverage in the 2012 Presidential Campaign and Beyond," *Politics & Policy* 40, No. 4: 547–556.

6. "Early Media Coverage Focuses on Horse Race," *PBS News Hour,* 12 June 2007.

7. Stephen Ansolabehere, Roy Behr, and Shanto Iyengar. 1992. *The Media Game: American Politics in the Television Age.* New York: Macmillan.

8. "Frames of Campaign Coverage," *Pew Research Center,* 23 April 2012, http://www.journalism.org/2012/04/23/frames-campaign-coverage.

9. Kiku Adatto. May 28, 1990. "The Incredible Shrinking Sound Bite," *New Republic* 202, No. 22: 20–23.

10. Erik Bucy and Maria Elizabeth Grabe. 2007. "Taking Television Seriously: A Sound and Image Bite Analysis of Presidential Campaign Coverage, 1992–2004," *Journal of Communication* 57, No. 4: 652–675.

11. Craig Fehrman, "The Incredible Shrinking Sound Bite," *Boston Globe,* 2 January 2011, http://www.boston.com/bostonglobe/ideas/articles/2011/01/02/the_incredible_shrinking_sound_bite/.

12. "Crossfire: Jon Stewart's America," *CNN,* 15 October 2004, http://www.cnn.com/TRANSCRIPTS/0410/15/cf.01.html.

13. Paul Begala, "Begala: The day Jon Stewart blew up my show," *CNN,* 12 February 2015.

14. Pew Research Center: Journalism & Media Staff, "Coverage of the Candidates by Media Sector and Cable Outlet," 1 November 2012.

"Winning the Media Campaign 2012," *Pew Research* Center, 2 November 2012.

15. Fred Greenstein. 2009. *The Presidential Difference*. Princeton, NJ: Princeton University Press.

16. "Dan Rather versus Richard Nixon, 1974," YouTube video, :46, from the National Association of Broadcasters annual convention in Houston on March 19,1974, posted by "thecelebratedmisterk," https://www.youtube.com/watch?v=ZGBLAKq8xwc (November 30, 2015); «'A Conversation With the President,' Interview With Dan Rather of the Columbia Broadcasting System,» *The American Presidency Project*, 2 January 1972, http://www.presidency.ucsb.edu/ws/?pid=3351.

17. Wolf Blitzer, "Dan Rather's Stand," *CNN*, 10 September 2004.

18. Matthew Eshbaugh-Soha and Jeffrey Peake. 2011. *Breaking Through the Noise: Presidential Leadership, Public Opinion, and the News Media*. Stanford, CA: Stanford University Press.

19. Ibid.

20. Gary Lee Malecha and Daniel J. Reagan. 2011. *The Public Congress: Congressional Deliberation in a New Media Age*. New York: Routledge.

21. Frank R. Baumgartner, Bryan D. Jones, and Beth L. Leech. 1997. "Media Attention and Congressional Agendas," In *Do The Media Govern? Politicians, Voters, and Reporters in America*, eds. Shanto Iyengar and Richard Reeves. Thousand Oaks, CA: Sage.

22. George Edwards and Dan Wood. 1999. "Who Influences Whom? The President, Congress, and the Media," *American Political Science Review* 93, No 2: 327–344; Yue Tan and David Weaver. 2007. «Agenda-Setting Effects Among the Media, the Public, and Congress, 1946–2004,» *Journalism & Mass Communication Quarterly* 84, No. 4: 729–745.

23. Ally Fogg, "Crime Is Falling. Now Let's Reduce Fear of Crime," *Guardian*, 24 April 24 2013.

24. Travis L. Dixon. 2008. "Crime News and Racialized Beliefs: Understanding the Relationship between Local News Viewing and Perceptions of African Americans and Crime," *Journal of Communication* 58, No. 1: 106–125.

25. Travis Dixon. 2015. "Good Guys Are Still Always in White? Positive Change and Continued Misrepresentation of Race and Crime on Local Television News," *Communication Research*, doi:10.1177/0093650215579223.

26. Travis L. Dixon. 2008. "Network News and Racial Beliefs: Exploring the Connection between National Television News Exposure and Stereotypical Perceptions of African Americans," *Journal of Communication* 58, No. 2: 321–337.

27. Martin Gilens. 1996. "Race and Poverty in America: Public Misperceptions and the American News Media," *Public Opinion Quarterly* 60, No. 4: 515–541.

28. Dixon. "Crime News and Racialized Beliefs."

29. Gilens. "Race and Poverty in America."

30. Shanto Iyengar and Donald R. Kinder. 1987. *News That Matters*. Chicago: University of Chicago Press.

31. Daniel C. Hallin. 2015. "The Dynamics of Immigration Coverage in Comparative Perspective," *American Behavioral Scientist* 59, No. 7: 876–885.

32. Kay Mills. 1996. "What Difference Do Women Journalists Make?" In *Women, the Media and Politics*, ed. Pippa Norris. Oxford, UK: Oxford University Press, 43.

33. Kim Fridkin Kahn and Edie N. Goldenberg. 1997. "The Media: Obstacle or Ally of Feminists?" In *Do the Media Govern?* eds. Shanto Iyengar and Richard Reeves. Thousand Oaks, CA: Sage.

34. Barbara Walters, "Ms. Walters Reflects," *Vanity Fair*, 31 May 2008. http://www.vanityfair.com/culture/2008/06/walters_excerpt200806

35. Mills. "What Difference Do Women Journalists Make?"

36. Mills. "What Difference Do Women Journalists Make?"

37. Kahn and Goldenberg, "The Media: Obstacle or Ally of Feminists?"

38. Kim Fridkin Kahn. 1994. "Does Gender Make a Difference? An Experimental Examination of Sex Stereotypes and Press Patterns in Statewide Campaigns," *American Journal of Political Science* 38, No. 1: 162–195.

39. John David Rausch, Mark Rozell, and Harry L. Wilson. 1999. "When Women Lose: A Study of Media Coverage of Two Gubernatorial Campaigns," *Women & Politics* 20, No. 4: 1–22.

40. Sarah Allen Gershon. 2013. "Media Coverage of Minority Congresswomen and Voter Evaluations: Evidence from an Online Experimental Study," *Political Research Quarterly* 66, No. 3: 702–714.

41. Jennifer Lawless and Richard Logan Fox. 2005. *It Takes a Candidate: Why Women Don't Run for Office.* Cambridge: Cambridge University Press.

42. Brittany L. Stalsburg, "Running with Strollers: The Impact of Family Life on Political Ambition," *Eagleton Institute of Politics*, Spring 2012, Unpublished Paper, http://www.eagleton.rutgers.edu/research/documents/Stalsburg-FamilyLife-Political-Ambition.pdf (August 28, 2015).

43. Christina Walker, "Is Sarah Palin Being Held to an Unfair Standard?" *CNN*, 8 September 2008.

44. Dana Bash, "Palin's Teen Daughter is Pregnant," *CNN*, 1 September 2008.

Jimmy Orr, "Palin Wardrobe Controversy Heightens - Todd is a Cheapo!" *Christian Science Monitor*, 26 October 2008.

14

Social Media Can Spread False Information

Phil Howard

Phil Howard is a writer for the Oxford Internet Institute, which is dedicated to the study of information, communication, and technology. It is part of the University of Oxford in England.

In the following viewpoint, Phil Howard questions if social media is killing democracy by discussing the amount of fake news and "clickbait" material that can be found in newsfeeds and timelines on social media. He also discusses the impact of bots, which are computer algorithms that can generate content in large masses and automatically publish it on social media. While Howard suggests the current state of politics in social media is hurting democracy, he finishes his viewpoint by suggesting that social media can also be used to save democracy once we learn how to evolve our technologies and eliminate fake news from our social media feeds.

This is the big year for computational propaganda—using immense data sets to manipulate public opinion over social media. Both the Brexit referendum and US election have revealed the limits of modern democracy, and social media platforms are currently setting those limits.

Platforms like Twitter and Facebook now provide a structure for our political lives. We've always relied on many kinds of sources for our political news and information. Family, friends, news

"Is Social Media Killing Democracy?" by Phil Howard, Culture Digitally, November 14, 2016. http://culturedigitally.org/2016/11/is-social-media-killing-democracy/. Reprinted by permission.

organizations, charismatic politicians certainly predate the internet. But whereas those are *sources* of information, social media now provides the *structure* for political conversation. And the problem is that these technologies permit too much fake news, encourage our herding instincts, and aren't expected to provide public goods.

First, social algorithms allow fake news stories from untrustworthy sources to spread like wildfire over networks of family and friends. Many of us just assume that there is a modicum of truth-in-advertising. We expect this from advertisements for commercial goods and services, but not from politicians and political parties. Occasionally a political actor gets punished for betraying the public trust through their misinformation campaigns. But in the United States "political speech" is completely free from reasonable public oversight, and in most other countries the media organizations and public offices for watching politicians are legally constrained, poorly financed, or themselves untrustworthy. Research demonstrates that during the campaigns for Brexit and the US Presidency large volumes of fake news stories, false factoids, and absurd claims were passed over social media networks, often by Twitter's highly automated accounts and Facebook's algorithms.

Second, social media algorithms provide very real structure to what political scientists often call "elective affinity" or "selective exposure." When offered the choice of who to spend time with or which organizations to trust, we prefer to strengthen our ties to the people and organizations we already know and like. When offered a choice of news stories, we prefer to read about the issues we already care about, from pundits and news outlets we've enjoyed in the past. Random exposure to content is gone from our diets of news and information. The problem is not that we have constructed our own community silos—humans will always do that. The problem is that social media networks take away the random exposure to new, high-quality information.

This is not a technological problem. We are social beings and so we will naturally look for ways to socialize, and we will use technology to socialize each other. But technology could be part of the solution. A not-so-radical redesign might occasionally expose us to new sources of information, or warn us when our own social networks are getting too bounded.

The third problem is that technology companies, including Facebook and Twitter, have been given a "moral pass" on the obligations we hold journalists and civil society groups to.

In most democracies, the public policy and exit polling systems have been broken for a decade. Many social scientists now find that big data, especially network data, does a better job of revealing public preferences than traditional random digit dial systems. So Facebook actually got a moral pass twice this year. Their data on public opinion would have certainly informed the Brexit debate, and their data on voter preferences would certainly have informed public conversation during the US election.

Facebook has run several experiments now, published in scholarly journals, demonstrating that they have the ability to accurately anticipate and measure social trends. Whereas journalists and social scientists feel an obligation to openly analyze and discuss public preferences, we do not expect this of Facebook. The network effects that clearly were unmeasured by pollsters were almost certainly observable to Facebook. When it comes to news and information about politics, or public preferences on important social questions, Facebook has a moral obligation to share data and prevent computational propaganda. The Brexit referendum and US election have taught us that Twitter and Facebook are now media companies. Their engineering decisions are effectively editorial decisions, and we need to expect more openness about how their algorithms work. And we should expect them to deliberate about their editorial decisions.

There are some ways to fix these problems. Opaque software algorithms shape what people find in their news feeds. We've all noticed fake news stories, often called clickbait, and while these can be an entertaining part of using the internet, it is bad when they are used to manipulate public opinion. These algorithms work as "bots" on social media platforms like Twitter, where they were used in both the Brexit and US Presidential campaign to aggressively advance the case for leaving Europe and the case for electing Trump. Similar algorithms work behind the scenes on Facebook, where they govern what content from your social networks actually gets your attention.

So the first way to strengthen democratic practices is for academics, journalists, policy makers and the interested public to audit social media algorithms. Was Hillary Clinton really replaced by an alien in the final weeks of the 2016 campaign? We all need to be able to see who wrote this story, whether or not it is true, and how it was spread. Most important, Facebook should not allow such stories to be presented as news, much less spread. If they take ad revenue for promoting political misinformation, they should face the same regulatory punishments that a broadcaster would face for doing such a public disservice.

The second problem is a social one that can be exacerbated by information technologies. This means it can also be mitigated by technologies. Introducing random news stories and ensuring exposure to high quality information would be a simple—and healthy—algorithmic adjustment to social media platforms. The third problem could be resolved with moral leadership from within social media firms, but a little public policy oversight from elections officials and media watchdogs would help. Did Facebook see that journalists and pollsters were wrong about public preferences? Facebook should have told us if so, and shared that data.

Social media platforms have provided a structure for spreading around fake news, we users tend to trust our friends and family, and we don't hold media technology firms accountable for degrading our public conversations. The next big thing for technology evolution is the Internet of Things, which will generate massive amounts of data that will further harden these structures. Is social media damaging democracy? Yes, but we can also use social media to save democracy.

15

The Power Behind Political Social Media Is Virality

Patrícia Rossini

Patrícia Rossini is a research associate and PhD candidate at the Syracuse University School of Information Studies.

In this viewpoint, Patrícia Rossini discusses the characteristics of social media content from 2016 presidential candidates that tended to draw the most attention and engagement from the public. This level of engagement was demonstrated by number of retweets on Twitter and number of times a post was "liked" on Facebook. She makes the argument that analyzing the public's reaction to candidates' posts on social media can enable politicians and their teams to better shape and adjust online campaign strategies.

Social media measures—likes, shares, retweets—are carefully tracked as ways to understand impact. For example, the Republican presidential nominee, Donald Trump, has over 11 million followers on Facebook and 12 million on Twitter. Hillary Clinton trails her celebrity rival, with 7 million on Facebook and just shy of 10 million followers on Twitter. These large follower numbers allow the candidates to reach beyond their own follower networks, through re-tweeting on Twitter and sharing on Facebook,

"Like, Re-Tweet, Repeat: Candidates' Top Messages on Social Media," by Patrícia Rossini, Illuminating 2016, November 8, 2016. http://illuminating.ischool.syr.edu/blog/view/top-messages. Licensed under CC BY 4.0.

to those of their followers, giving the candidates even greater visibility and impact.

Metrics such as Facebook's likes and Twitter's re-tweets are important for campaign managers to understand the type of content that resonates with their audience. Because re-tweets and likes are relevant features for the social media ecosystem, Illuminating 2016 features the current five top re-tweeted messages and the five most liked Facebook messages during the campaign so far. In this blog post, we take a closer look at this feature to understand what types of messages are most like to be retweeted on Twitter and shared on Facebook.

What we find is that even though attack messages are not the main type of messaging used by Trump on social media, most of his top retweeted and shared messages on Twitter and Facebook are attacks on opponents, the news media, and others. Conversely, although Clinton produces sometimes as much as 1.5 times as many messages on social media compared to Trump, she is much less likely to appear in the top five most retweeted or shared posts. This is because she generally had been getting fewer of these engagement behaviors with her social media in the three months we did this analysis. The Republican candidate enjoyed more popularity on both social media platforms, generating 42 out of 65 (64%) top re-tweeted messages and 53 out of 65 top liked posts, (81%).

We analyzed 130 messages featured at the Illuminating 2016 website during 13 weeks, from August 1st to October 31th—covering the post-primary phase that marks the official presidential campaign period.

Going Negative

When looking at message types, the overall view shared by journalists and citizens that Trump's campaign is negative on social media becomes clear. In fact, 57% of his top re-tweeted messages are attacks, which suggests that adopting a negative tone resonates well with his audience.

Moreover, when Trump goes negative, he is mostly targeting his opponent's image. That was the case for 79% of his attacks. When posting positive messages to advocate for his own candidacy, Trump also tends to focus on his image: 66% of his advocacy top-tweets are focused on building his character.

Clinton's top re-tweeted messages are also more negative. Roughly 60% of her featured tweets are attacking Trump. Another interesting fact is that the Democratic candidate shifts her focus when attacking and advocating. For negative messages, her main focus is Trump's image, the focus of 10 out of 14 attacks. For advocacy posts, the emphasis is evenly distributed between character-building and her positions on the issues—corroborating our prior analysis on the primaries that the Democratic candidate is more likely to focus on issues than her Republican opponent.

Different Platforms, Different Messages

On Facebook, likes can be seen as a barometer of public reactions towards candidates' messages. Unlike re-tweets, likes do not necessarily increase a message's visibility. However, likes express an affinity or a reaction to a Facebook post and may contribute to enhancing its organic reach—that is, the probability of a post appearing on the Facebook wall of users who like the page without being sponsored.

For Donald Trump, the most liked messages are evenly distributed between posts advocating for himself and those attacking his opponent, her party or her surrogates, with 26% each. Like on Twitter, most of his advocacy and attack messages are image-focused (78%). In other words, his posts that either advocate for him on his image or attack his opponent's image are liked more than policy posts.

Hillary Clinton had twelve featured messages within the 13-week period. Her message types were somewhat evenly distributed, with Advocacy, Calls to Action and Ceremonial accounting for 25% each.

Social media provides valuable for campaigns to analyze, shape and adjust communicative strategies online. In this blog post, we analyzed the type of content that draws attention and promotes engagement of Clinton's and Trump's supporters by looking at the top-retweeted and top-liked messages on Twitter and Facebook.

Negative messages are by far the most featured message type for both candidates, which suggests that the overall negative tone of the 2016 elections is also resonating well among Clinton's and Trump's supporters. As for the focus of these messages, our analysis corroborates previous findings, demonstrating that image is the main target of Donald Trump's top messages—either to attack or to advocate for himself. Despite the fact that Clinton is generally more focused on issues, when it comes to top messages, her featured attacks are also focused on image.

Even though top re-tweets and top-likes do not present a clear picture of what campaigns are doing on social media, they are relevant insofar as they demonstrate what type of messaging promote citizen engagement and may help shape campaign communication. In this sense, as this electoral cycle is being frequently labeled as "the most negative campaign" of America's recent history, it is not surprising that attacks are also the most used type of messaging in candidates' top-retweeted and top liked messages on social media.

16

Social Media Can't Fix World Politics

Rania Fakhoury

Rania Fakhoury is an associate researcher for LaRIFA at Lebanese University. She holds a doctorate in Business Administration (DBA).

In the following viewpoint, Rania Fakhoury discusses whether social media can fix world politics, analyzing both its positive and negative aspects. The positive include social media's ability to provide people with a platform to participate in government affairs and start conversations, but on the negative side social media allows for a more transparent view of the pitfalls that sometimes are a part of politics. Fakhoury also looks at politics around the world and the ways in which social media allows the public to see what is happening in the political landscape in other countries besides their own.

P rivacy is no longer a social norm, said Facebook founder Mark Zuckerberg in 2010, as social media took a leap to bring more private information into the public domain.

But what does it mean for governments, citizens and the exercise of democracy? Donald Trump is clearly not the first leader to use his Twitter account as a way to both proclaim his policies and influence the political climate. Social media presents novel challenges to strategic policy, and has become a managerial issues for many governments.

But it also offers a free platform for public participation in government affairs. Many argue that the rise of social media

"Can social media, loud and inclusive, fix world politics?" by Rania Fakhoury, The Conversation, February 20, 2017. https://theconversation.com/can-social-media-loud-and-inclusive-fix-world-politics-74287. Licensed Under CC BY-ND 4.0 International.

technologies can give citizens and observers a better opportunity to identify pitfalls of government and their politics.

As governments embrace the role of social media and the influence of negative or positive feedback on the success of their project, they are also using this tool to their advantages by spreading fabricated news.

This much freedom of expression and opinion can be a double-edged sword.

A Tool that Triggers Change

On the positive side, social media include social networking applications such as Facebook and Google+, microblogging services such as Twitter, blogs, video blogs (vlogs), wikis, and media-sharing sites such as YouTube and Flickr, among others.

Social media as a collaborative and participatory tool, connects users with each other and help shaping various communities. Playing a key role in delivering public service value to citizens it also helps people to engage in politics and policy-making, making processes easier to understand, through information and communication technologies (ICTs).

Today four out of five countries in the world have social media features on their national portals to promote interactive networking and communication with the citizen. Although we don't have any information about the effectiveness of such tools or whether they are used to their full potential, 20% of these countries shows that they have "resulted in new policy decisions, regulation or service."

Social media can be an effective tool to trigger changes in government policies and services if well used. It can be used to prevent corruption, as it is direct method of reaching citizens. In developing countries, corruption is often linked to governmental services that lack automated processes or transparency in payments.

The UK is taking the lead on this issue. Its anti-corruption innovation hub aims to connect several stakeholders—including civil society, law enforcement and technologies experts—to engage their efforts toward a more transparent society.

With social media, governments can improve and change the way they communicate with their citizens—and even question government projects and policies. In Kazakhstan, for example, a migration-related legislative amendment entered into force early January 2017 and compelled property owners to register people residing in their homes immediately or else face a penalty charge starting in February 2017.

Citizens were unprepared for this requirement, and many responded with indignation on social media. At first the government ignored this reaction. However, as the growing anger soared via social media, the government took action and introduced a new service to facilitate the registration of temporary citizens.

Shaping Political Discourse

Increasing digital services have engaged and encouraged the public to become more socially responsible and politically involved. But many governments are wary of the power that technology, and most specifically smart media, exerts over citizens' political involvement.

Popular social media platforms like Facebook, Twitter and WhatsApp are being censored by many governments. China, South Africa and others are passing laws to regulate the social media sphere.

The dominance of social media allows citizens to have quick access to government information—information whose legitimacy may not be validated. As this happens, the organic image formed in their minds will be affected and changed and an induced image, whether negative or positive, will be formulated.

For example, the top trending topics on social media right now are related to a tweet from WikiLeaks claiming that CIA can get into smart electronics—like iPhones and Samsung TVs—to spy on individuals. This series of revelations led WikiLeaks founder Julian Assange to see his internet access cut off, allegedly by the government of Ecuador, in October 2016.

For his supporters, this step jeopardises what they perceive as the voice of truth. WikiLeaks usually spread mass of sensitive and reliable information into the public domain about politics, society and the economy.

Others state that confidential information should not be published in social media because it might endanger life and could be misinterpreted.

In 2011, social media played a crucial role in the direction of the Arab Spring in Egypt, Tunisia and Libya, enabling protesters in those countries to share information and disclose the atrocities committed by their own governments. This ignited a "domino effect" that led to mass revolts.

Governments reacted by trying to impose draconian restrictions on social media, from censorship to promoting fake news and propaganda against them.

The dissemination of uncensored information through social media has precipitated a wave of public shows of dissatisfaction, characterised by a mix of demands for better public services, changes in the institutions and instating a socially-legitimated state. Citizens use social media to meet up and interact with different groups, and some of those encounters lead to concrete actions.

Where's the Long-Term Fix?

But the campaigns that result do not always evolve into positive change.

Egypt and Libya are still facing several major crises over the last years, along with political instability and domestic terrorism. The social media influence that triggered the Arab Spring did not permit these political systems to turn from autocracy to democracy.

Brazil exemplifies a government's failure to react properly to a massive social media outburst. In June 2013 people took to the streets to protest the rising fares of public transportation. Citizens channelled their anger and outrage through social media to mobilise networks and generate support.

The Brazilian government didn't understand that "the message is the people." Though the riots some called the "Tropical Spring" disappeared rather abruptly in the months to come, they had major and devastating impact on Brazil's political power, culminating in the impeachment of President Rousseff in late 2016 and the worst recession in Brazil's history.

As in the Arab Spring countries, the use of social media in Brazil did not result in economic improvement. The country has tumbled down into depression, and unemployment has risen to 12.6%.

Extremism, Fake News and Hate Speech

Social media is also used to propagate "fake news" in order to destabilise an organisation or a country. The spread of disinformation through social media shows how governments can use the art of communication to channel specific facts to their own citizens—or to the world.

In 2014, Russia spread conspiracy theories and fake stories, both during the Crimea crisis and the downing of Malaysia Airlines Flight 17, to hide its military involvement in Ukraine. More recently, the Kremlin (or its agents) manipulated social media to spread "fake news" and pro-Trump messages during the American presidential election. The objective of this digital disinformation campaign was to shake the American political system, rather than to change the results of the election.

Social media also provide a powerful platform for extremism and hate speech, citizen activities that should compel government action.

Social media may have been used for extreme purposes, to topple presidents, spread calumny, and meddle in internal affairs of foreign countries. But it remains a potent technological tool that governments can use to capture and understand the needs and preferences of their citizens, and to engage them, on their own terms from the very beginning of the process as agencies develop public services.

Governments typically asks "how can we adapt social media to the way in which we do e-services," and then try to shape their policies accordingly. They would be wiser to ask, "how can social media enable us to do things differently in a way they've never been done before?"—that is, policy-making in collaboration with people.

17

Trolling, Tribalism, and Performance on Social Media

Lam Thuy Vo

Lam Thuy Vo is a senior reporter at BuzzFeed News. *She focuses on data-driven reportage about economics, social issues, and web culture.*

In this viewpoint, Lam Thuy Vo argues that social media has changed the way we live our lives, and that this is especially clear in the political realm. She traces some of the major changes that have taken place with the rise of social media, including more direct access to politicians and their ideological mindset, increased trolling and combative behavior in political discourse, and increased tribalism in the political as well as the social realm. Furthermore, she offers suggestions for how to improve social media and information literacy, which she argues will help people to become less vulnerable to the misinformation and manipulation that is rampant on social media.

I t's become crucial for reporters to gain a better grasp of the social web. Recent revelations around Russian interference with the 2016 presidential elections and Donald Trump's Twitter-heavy way of governing the US show that there's an ever-growing need to develop literacy around the usefulness and pitfalls of social media data.

Our lives online are no longer just mere extensions of the happenings in our lives in the "real world." We make connections online—good ones and bad—and have experiences online that feel real and formative. We build our world views based on information we are exposed to online. Our *umwelt* has expanded into the virtual realm.

Now, we also understand, the social web has increasingly become a space where economically and politically motivated actors game virality for personal gain.

During the BuzzFeed Open Lab fellowship, which wrapped last week, I wanted to investigate this space with code. I wanted to find programmatic ways to explore social media data and develop a deeper understanding of how it can help—and potentially obfuscate—stories that journalists pursue. Below are some of the story archetypes and issues I've discovered along the way.

A Megaphone for Politicians and Everyday People

Privacy lives on a scale rather than a binary—what we consider private and public changes with each audience. What I share with my best friend is different from what I share with my mother, which is different from what I share with colleagues, students, or neighbors.

Online, this scale is distorted. This results in online behavior that can be both deeply personal and performative at the same time. Everything we post for more than one person—on private or public forums, our timelines, our Twitter account—is sort of public, yet directed towards a semi-personal audience, who may or may not listen.

For public figures and everyday people alike, social media has become a way to address the public in a direct manner. Status updates, tweets, and posts can serve as ways to bypass older projection mechanisms like the news media or press releases. And so what we do online—or who we say we *are* online—should always be taken with a grain of salt. It's what we project to be, perhaps an imagination of our ideal self.

For politicians, however, these public announcements—these projections of their selves—may become binding statements, and in the case of powerful political figures may become harbingers for policies that have yet to be put in place.

Because a politician's job is partially to be public-facing, researching a politician's social media accounts can help us better understand their ideological mindset. For one story, my colleague Charlie Warzel and I collected and analyzed more than 20,000 of Donald Trump's tweets to answer the following question: what kind of information does he disseminate and how can this information serve as a proxy for the kind of information he may consume?

Social data points are not a full image of who we actually are, in part due to its performative nature and in part because these data sets are incomplete and so open to individual interpretation. But they *can* help as complements: President Trump's affiliation with Breitbart online, as shown above, was an early indicator for his strong ties to Steve Bannon in real life. His retweeting of smaller conservative blogs like theconservativetreehouse. com and newsninja2012.com perhaps hinted at his distrust of "mainstream media."

The lesson here is that public statements on social media are interesting indicators of how people project themselves to others, especially for public figures, but should be complementary with other reporting and interpreted with caution.

A Stage for (Emotional) Experiences

Many of our interactions are moving exclusively onto online platforms. As our lives become more tethered to online platforms, we become more vulnerable and emotionally attached to what happens on them.

In other words, what happens to us on the internet *does* matter, regardless of how it may or may not manifest itself in the real world. Social behavior online often mirrors social behavior offline—except that online, human beings are assisted by powerful tools.

Take bullying, for instance. Bullying has arguably existed as long as humankind. But now bullies are assisted by thousands of other bullies that can be called upon in the blink of an eye. Bullies have access to search engines and digital traces of a person's life, sometimes going as far back as that person's online personas go. And they have the means of amplification—one bully shouting from across the hallway is not nearly as deafening as thousands of them coming atcha all at the same time.

Such is the nature of trolling.

Washington Post editor Doris Truong, for instance, found herself at the heart of a political controversy online. Over the course of a few days, trolls (and a good number of people defending her) directed 24,731 Twitter mentions at her. Being pummeled with vitriol on the internet can only be ignored for so long before it takes some kind of emotional toll.

Social Dynamics and How to Game Them

We are also starting to see the emergence of social structures—the formation of "in-crowds" and "out-crowds." Internet culture is optimized and visually designed to encourage quick and emotional sharing, not thoughtful, nuanced discussions. This means that people are encouraged to jump into the fray based on whatever outrage/joy they feel. There's little incentive online to slow down, to read beyond headlines, and to take the time to digest before we join our respective ideological crowds in cheering on or expressing our discontent with a certain issue.

Human beings are tribal at their core. It's easy to follow the urge to fall into groups that affirm our views. Algorithms only steer us further into those corners.

For one story, we analyzed the Facebook newsfeeds of a conservative mother and her liberal daughter. We found that not only were the groups and pages they followed completely different but the friends who showed up on their feeds also differed entirely.

Both mother and daughter were surprised at just how different their newsfeeds were, given that they both grew up in the same places, love and care about many of the same people, and share a lot of values outside of the realm of politics. They found that their experience online was more divisive than their face-to-face encounters were.

Automation, Bots & Cyborgs

Social platforms play to our adherence to "our tribes" and has us gathering in large groups around specific subjects. Where there's a lot of eyeballs there's money to be made and influence to be wielded. Enter the new players in this realm: (semi-)automated accounts like bots and *cyborgs*.

Bots are not evil from the get-go: there are plenty of bots that may delight us with their whimsical haikus or self-care tips. But as Atlantic Council fellow Ben Nimmo, who has researched bot armies for years, told me for one story: "[Bots] have the potential to seriously distort any debate [...] They can make a group of six people look like a group of 46,000 people."

The social media platforms themselves are at a pivotal point in their existence where they have to recognize their responsibility in defining and clamping down on what they may deem a "problematic bot." In the meantime, journalists should recognize the ever-growing presence of non-humans and their power online.

Moving Forward

Many phenomena—from trolling to online tribalism—had previously been observed before this election, but were often painted as events that happened on the fringes of the web. Now people are talking about how misinformation campaigns may imperil elections worldwide; about how filter bubbles could be skewing billions of people's points of view; and about how online hate campaigns may impact just about anyone.

With this in mind it seems imperative to better understand the universe of social data. This includes developing a data literacy just around the social web. Some of the main takeaways from this research may be broadly structured as follows:

Issues Surrounding Problematic Automation

Not every user is a person; there are automated accounts (bots) and accounts that are semi-automated and semi-human controlled (cyborgs). As mentioned above, not every bot or cyborg is bad, but those that are deployed en masse may be used to skew how we should view political issues or events. Ever-more important tasks include: understanding what kind of user behavior indicates automation, what motivations lie behind their creation, and the scope of their capabilities.

The Tyranny of the Loudest

Not everything or everyone's behavior is measured. A vast amount of people choose to remain silent. An analysis of a video live stream of one of President Trump's speeches revealed that only 2–3 percent of those viewing the stream chose to comment or react to it. 97 percent were silent.

What this means is that the content that Facebook, Twitter and other platforms algorithmically surface on our social feeds is often based on the likes, retweets and comments of those who chose to chime in. Those who did not speak up are disproportionately drowned out in this process. Therefore, we need to be as mindful of what *is not* measured as we are understand what conclusions we can draw from the limited social data of what *is* measured.

We Are the Product, Hence Our Data Is Not Ours

Our data is what makes Facebook, Twitter and other social media platforms valuable. Every click and like, even our searches and posts, contribute to a massive corpus of data that is more valuable than any marketing research could ever be. It's longitudinal data about our behavior and, more importantly, indicators of how we feel about issues, people, and—dare I say it—products. By using social platforms, we opt into giving them power over our data, and they decide how much access we get to it. In many cases that's very little. This means that we have to find ways to better that is provided by these companies. It also means journalists may need to be more creative in how they report and tell these stories—journalists may want to buy bots to better understand how they act online, or reporters may want to purchase Facebook ads to get a better understanding of how Facebook works. Whatever the means, operating within and outside of the confines set by social media companies will be a major challenge for journalists as they are navigating this ever-changing cyber environment.

I will continue to explore the social web beyond this fellowship here at *BuzzFeed News* as a reporter. My research will continue to be updated here, and I'm in the process of writing an instructional coding book to teach novices how to navigate data mining on social media platforms. Please feel free to get in touch.

Organizations to Contact

The editors have compiled the following list of organizations concerned with the issues debated in this book. The descriptions are derived from materials provided by the organizations. All have publications or information available for interested readers. The list was compiled on the date of publication of the present volume; the information provided here may change. Be aware that many organizations take several weeks or longer to respond to inquiries, so allow as much time as possible.

Digital Media Association (DiMA)
1050 17th Street, NW
Suite 520
Washington, DC 20036
phone: (202) 639-9509
website: www.digmedia.org

DiMA is the ambassador for the digital media industry: webcasters, online media, digital services, and technology innovators. DiMA is the leading advocate for a stable legal environment in which to build ideas into industries, and inventions into profits.

Elway Research, Inc.
Seattle, WA 98103
phone: (206) 264-1500
email: elway@elwayresearch.com
website: www.elwayresearch.com

Elway Research, Inc. is a polling organization that conducts research and public opinion studies for a variety of clients, including political parties. According to its website, fivethirtyeight.com rated it one of the top six pollsters in the country.

FactCheck.org
Annenberg Public Policy Center
202 S. 36th St.
Philadelphia, PA 19104-3806
phone: (215) 898-9400
email: editor@factcheck.org
website: www.factcheck.org

FactCheck.org is a project of the Annenberg Public Policy Center of the University of Pennsylvania. It is a nonpartisan, nonprofit "consumer advocate" for voters that aims to reduce the level of deception and confusion in US politics. They monitor the factual accuracy of what is said by major US political players in the form of TV ads, debates, speeches, interviews, and news releases.

Media Literacy Now
15 Main Street, Suite 102
Watertown, MA 02472
phone: (617) 395-4222
email: info@medialiteracynow.org
website: www.medialiteracynow.org

Media Literacy Now is a nonprofit organization focused on promoting policy change at the state and national level to ensure all students receive comprehensive media literacy education and skills. It empowers grassroots groups and individuals to push for changes in their local school district's curriculum. The organization also provides policy and advocacy information and resources to develop state laws for the implementation of media literacy education in schools.

National Scholastic Press Association
2829 University Ave. SE, Suite 720
Minneapolis, MN 55414
phone: (612) 200-9254
email: info@studentpress.org
website: http://studentpress.org

The National Scholastic Press Association is a nonprofit educational service dedicated to providing journalism education sources. It utilizes education training and recognition programs for members to promote the standards and ethics of good journalism as accepted and practiced by print, broadcast, and electronic media in the United States.

Nielsen
85 Broad St.
New York, NY 10004
phone: (646) 654-5000
website: www.nielsen.com

Nielsen is a global measurement and data analytics company that provides complete views of consumers and markets worldwide. In 1950, Nielsen officially moved its focus to television, in which it currently uses an audience measurement system to determine ratings and audience sizes of television programming in the US.

Nonprofit VOTE
2464 Massachusetts Ave., Suite 210
Cambridge, MA 02140
phone: (617) 357-8683
email: info@nonprofitvote.org
website: www.nonprofitvote.org

Nonprofit VOTE is a nonpartisan, nonprofit organization that helps the participants of other nonprofits in the US vote. The organization was founded in 2005 and offers training to other nonprofit networks on how to drive voter participation.

Pew Research Center
1615 L Street, NW
Suite 800
Washington, DC 20036
phone: (202) 419-4300
email: info@pewresearch.org
website: www.pewresearch.org

The Pew Research Center is a nonpartisan organization that informs the public about issues and information that shape the world. The Pew Research Center conducts a lot of research and polls to align facts and data.

Project Looksharp
1119 Williams Hall
Ithaca, NY 14850-7290
phone: (607) 274-3471
email: looksharp@ithaca.edu
website: www.projectlooksharp.org/

Project Looksharp is a media literacy organization provided by Ithaca College. It works with educators by offering lesson plans, media materials, training, and support for the integration of media literacy into classroom curricula. Part of Project Looksharp's curriculum involves teaching students how to evaluate news articles.

Scholars Strategy Network
675 Massachusetts Avenue, 8th Floor
Cambridge, MA 02139
phone: (617) 333-8205
website: www.scholarsstrategynetwork.org

The Scholars Strategy Network is largely made up of university based scholars who donate their time in addition to a small professional staff. The organization focuses on improving public policy and democracy by connecting scholars and research to policymakers and the media.

Bibliography

Books

Craig Agranoff and Herbert Tabin, *Socially Elected: How To Win Elections Using Social Media*. Grand Junction, CO: Pendant Publishing, 2011.

Axel Bruns, Gunn Enli, Eli Skogerbo, Anders Olof Larsson, Christian Christensen, *The Routledge Companion to Social Media and Politics*. Philadelphia, PA: Taylor & Francis, 2015.

Andrea Ceron, Luigi Curini, and Stefano Maria Iacus, *Politics and Big Data: Nowcasting and Forecasting Elections with Social Media*. Philadelphia, PA: Taylor & Francis, 2017.

Andrea Ceron, *Social Media and Political Accountability: Bridging the Gap between Citizens and Politicians*. New York, NY: Springer, 2017.

Victoria A. Farrar-Myers and Justin S. Vaughn, *Controlling the Message: New Media in American Political Campaigns*. New York, NY: NYU Press, 2015.

Jason Gainous and Kevin M. Wagner, *Tweeting to Power: The Social Media Revolution in American Politics*. New York, NY: Oxford University Press, 2013.

Tim Highfield, *Social Media and Everyday Politics / Edition 1*. Hoboken, NJ: Wiley, 2016.

James Katz, Michael Barris, and Anshul Jain, *The Social Media President: Barack Obama and the Politics of Digital Engagement*. London, England: Palgrave Macmillan UK, 2013.

Helen Margetts, Peter John, Scott Hale, and Taha Yasseri, *Political Turbulence: How Social Media Shape Collective Action*. Princeton, NJ: Princeton University Press, 2015.

Bogdan Patrut and Monica Patrut, *Social Media in Politics: Case Studies on the Political Power of Social Media*. New York, NY: Springer, 2016.

Joel Penney. *The Citizen Marketer: Promoting Political Opinion in the Social Media Age*, New York, NY: Oxford University Press, 2017.

Glenn W. Richardson Jr., *Social Media and Politics [2 volumes]: A New Way to Participate in the Political Process*. Santa Barbara, CA: ABC-CLIO, Incorporated, 2016.

Greg Strandberg, *Social Media Politics: Using the Internet to Get Elected*. CreateSpace Publishing, 2015.

Cass R. Sunstein, *#Republic: Divided Democracy in the Age of Social Media*. Princeton, NJ: Princeton University Press, 2017.

Andrew White, *Digital Media and Society: Transforming Economics, Politics and Social Practices*. London, England: Palgrave Macmillan UK, 2014.

Periodicals and Internet Sources

Monica Anderson, "More Americans are using social media to connect with politicians," Pew Research Center, May 19, 2015, http://www.pewresearch.org/fact-tank/2015/05/19/more-americans-are-using-social-media-to-connect-with-politicians/.

Natalie Andrews, "Senators to Pitch Bill Regulating Political Ads on Social Media," *Wall Street Journal*, October 4, 2017, https://www.wsj.com/articles/political-ads-on-social-media-could-face-more-regulation-1507146803.

Jonah Bromwich, "Social Media Is Not Contributing Significantly to Political Polarization, Paper Says," *New York Times*, April 13, 2017, https://www.nytimes.com/2017/04/13/us/political-polarization-internet.html.

Philip Bump, "How politicians' use of social media is reinforcing a partisan media divide," *Washington Post*, December 18, 2017, https://www.washingtonpost.com/news/politics/wp/2017/12/18/how-politicians-use-of-social-media-is-reinforcing-a-partisan-media-divide/?utm_term=.aeb3ff6a03de.

Dylan Byers, "After Russian Facebook ads, Democrats seek new FEC rules on social media politics," *CNN*, September 20, 2017, http://money.cnn.com/2017/09/19/media/congress-facebook-fec/index.html.

Benedict Carey, "How Fiction Becomes Fact on Social Media," *New York Times*, October 20, 2017, https://www.nytimes.com/2017/10/20/health/social-media-fake-news.html.

Wesley Donehue, "The danger of Twitter, Facebook politics," *CNN*, April 24, 2012, http://www.cnn.com/2012/04/24/opinion/donehue-social-media-politics/index.html.

Juliet Eilperin, "Here's how the first president of the social media age has chosen to connect with Americans," *Washington Post*, May 26, 2015, https://www.washingtonpost.com/news/politics/wp/2015/05/26/heres-how-the-first-president-of-the-social-media-age-has-chosen-to-connect-with-americans/?utm_term=.2035dbd67eb9.

Erin Kelly, "Senators unveil bipartisan bill to reveal who is buying political ads on social media," *USA Today*, October 19, 2017, https://www.usatoday.com/story/news/politics/2017/10/19/senators-introduce-bipartisan-bill-aimed-social-mediato-require-online-political-ads-disclose-fundin/780250001/.

Ezra Klein, "Something is breaking American politics, but it's not social media," *Vox*, April 12, 2017, https://www.vox.com/policy-and-politics/2017/4/12/15259438/social-media-political-polarization.

Tom McCarthy, "How Russia used social media to divide Americans," *Guardian*, October 14, 2017, https://www.theguardian.com/us-news/2017/oct/14/russia-us-politics-social-media-facebook.

David Nield, "Social media and the future of elections," *Telegraph*, March 1, 2017, http://www.telegraph.co.uk/connect/better-business/social-media-and-the-future-of-elections/.

Steven Overly, "Your political posts on social media are actually changing minds—sometimes," *Washington Post*, November 7, 2016, https://www.washingtonpost.com/news/innovations/wp/2016/11/07/your-political-posts-on-social-media-are-actually-changing-minds-sometimes-2/?utm_term=.c6fdcb327697.

Dan Patterson, "Election Tech: Why social media is more powerful than advertising," *TechRepublic*, May 31, 2016, https://www.techrepublic.com/article/election-tech-why-social-media-is-more-powerful-than-advertising/.

Jim Warren, "Social media influences politics, but not in the way you might think," *Toronto Sun*, October 14, 2017, http://torontosun.com/2017/10/14/social-media-influences-politics-but-not-in-the-way-you-might-think/wcm/5f75f8df-3f78-46da-a3ff-94c233c2fbaf.

Index